small LOOM
& freeform
weaving

five ways to weave

++++++++++++++++++++++++++++++++++++++

Barbara Matthiessen

Creative Publishing
international

Creative Publishing international

First published in the United States of America by
Creative Publishing international, Inc., a member of
Quayside Publishing Group
400 First Avenue North
Suite 300
Minneapolis, MN 55401
1-800-328-3895
www.creativepub.com

ISBN-13: 978-1-58923-361-4
ISBN-10: 1-58923-361-1

10 9 8 7 6 5 4 3 2 1

Library of Congress Cataloging-in-Publication Data
Matthiessen, Barbara.
  Small loom and freeform weaving : five ways to weave / Barbara Matthiessen.
     p. cm.
  ISBN 1-58923-361-1
  1. Hand weaving. 2. Handlooms. I. Title.

TT848.M3835 2008
746.1'4--dc22   2007049018
                                                 CIP

Copy Editor: Julia Maranan
Proofreader: Carol Polakowski
Book Design: Rachel Fitzgibbon
Cover Design: everlution design
Page Layout: Rachel Fitzgibbon
Illustrations: Michael Wanke
Photographs: Ned Witrodgen

Printed in China

CONTENTS

INTRODUCTION

Weaving just might be our most ancient art form and undoubtedly the most common and useful. Baskets, braids, and cloth have been woven from indigenous plant materials and animal hair for thousands of years in all cultures. In these cultures, weaving has supplied a multitude of items from containers and clothing to decorative elements of comfort and beauty.

Gorgeous yarns, fibers, and wool seduce me—I love the way they feel and look. Weaving allows me to justify my compulsion by making fun, practical, and pleasing projects for my home, family, friends, and myself. Working with these materials is relaxing, rewarding, and easier than you might imagine.

For those of you already working with yarns and fibers, weaving will be easy to add to your skill set since many of the tools, terms, and techniques are also used in knitting, crocheting, and needlework. Novice yarn enthusiasts will be delighted to see that there are few necessary tools to purchase to get started on this adventure. Weaving truly has something to offer to everyone.

Small looms, such as those used in this book, are ideal to introduce the joys of weaving and are practical for many smaller-scale projects. They are portable and inexpensive, yet produce wonderful goods. You can also create your own looms with flat boards and hair combs, or use pins and foam-core board for a method called pin weaving. With a little imagination, you'll discover that you can weave freeform directly onto many natural and hand-fashioned frameworks, like a bicycle rim, a wire artist's easel, or a simple arrangement of nails pounded into a board. Each loom style or weaving method has its own advantages; however, many of the projects can be done on more than one loom with simple adaptations.

Most of the projects in this book can be done in an evening or during a weekend, which makes them perfect to jazz up an outfit or for last-minute gifts. You might even be able to use up yarn left over from other projects, making these FREE! From super-simple to artsy/funky, there is a project here for everyone who wants to try their hand at weaving.

GETTING STARTED

DESIGN BASICS

What is the first step when designing for weaving? Determining the function. You need to consider the end use of the project in the very beginning of the design process. By recognizing the limits, or lack of limits, for your particular project, you will make better choices throughout the design process.

Ask yourself some questions: Does this project need to be washable? How much durability do I need? What feel or drape do I need for this project? Will this be an art piece with no limits?

When choosing materials, be sure to read their labels for fiber content and laundering instructions. You really do not want to weave a cardigan that cannot be washed! On the other hand, wall hangings that are only occasionally vacuumed can utilize almost any material. For more on choosing materials, refer to Weaving Materials (page 20).

Ideally, a design will marry texture, color, and form into a pleasing combination. Here's how each of these elements applies to weaving.

Texture

Texture is one of the most apparent characteristics of weaving, and the easiest to produce. Two choices, material and stitch or pattern, can determine whether the texture has a smooth, even finish or if it's lumpy, bumpy, or fluffy. Smooth materials and a balanced weave produce the smoothest finish and make lovely linens and delightful-to-wear goods. Lumpy, bumpy, and fluffy textures are made using textured materials along with a variety of stitches, such as Rya and Soumak. These deep textures work well on tapestries and art pieces and as accents on wearable and home décor pieces.

One way to learn about texture is to create a sampler using a variety of materials and stitches. Making a sampler will also give you an idea as to warp tension, interplay of warp with weft, and a feel for the process that will assist you when designing. After you have read this Basics section, warp up a flat loom and experiment using materials that you have on hand, mixing in some of the stitches from this book. Play, and you will learn a great deal about the process.

Color

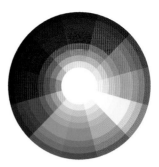

Color tends to be the feature that first draws us in, but it can also be the most confusing when designing for weaving. There are many theories about the use of color, but here is an overview of the basics:

Hue is pure color and the name of the family on the color spectrum. Red, pink, and burgundy are in the same color family.

Value is the amount of lightness or darkness in a color family. Pink is a light value of red.

Intensity is the brightness or dullness of a color. A color is most intense when it is closest to the pure color, as in bright red.

No discussion about color can leave out the color wheel and its importance in the language of design. Briefly, here are some color wheel terms you may find helpful:

Primary colors are pure colors from which all other colors are created. They are red, yellow, and blue.

Secondary colors are a mix of two primary colors (for example, orange is a blend of red and yellow). Secondary colors are orange, purple, and green.

Tertiary colors are made by mixing adjacent primary and secondary colors. Blue-green, red-orange, yellow-orange, red-purple, blue-purple, and yellow-green are the tertiary colors.

Complements are colors opposite each other on the color wheel. Red and green are an example. If you mix two complementary colors, you will make gray. To dull the intensity of a color, add a bit of its complement.

Monochromatic means two or more values of a single hue. Red and pink are considered monochromatic.

Analogous colors are next to each other on the color wheel. Yellow, orange, and red are analogous.

Other useful terms are:

Tint adding white to any hue
Shade adding black to any hue
Tone adding gray to any hue

One way to think about color in weaving is to relate it to pixels or to the pointillism style of painting. The effect up close can be quite different from the overall appearance from even a few feet away. The warp and weft colors intertwine so the eye perceives this blended color.

The amount of each color and its texture also affect how it is perceived. Adding multiple textures of the same hue increases its interest. The bulk or thickness of a material affects the color balance when teamed with a less bulky material.

COLOR TIPS AND IDEAS

- Monochromatic color schemes are calming and elegant. Add a variety of textures to keep them interesting.

- Be careful of complementary color schemes unless you want a grayed appearance. Consider mixing in a neutral color to offset the graying effect.

- Mix yarn or fibers while weaving to give the effect of a third color. For example, twist yellow and red together for an orange look.

- White warp will tone down colors, while black adds sparkle.

- Learning about and experimenting with color is a worthwhile activity for all your artistic endeavors.

LOOMS

The projects in this book were produced on a variety of small looms, some purchased and others easily made at home. Each loom style has its own advantages. Because each loom offers me something different, I cannot say I have a favorite—they are like children, each different and charming in its own way.

One of the beautiful aspects about weaving is that you can start out with a few very simple tools. Many of the tools, such as scissors and a measuring tape or ruler, you probably already possess. Other handy items are masking tape, clothespins, and a variety of yarn or tapestry needles.

Here are definitions of common terms that appear throughout this book:

WARP The lengthwise material attached to the loom. Warping is attaching the warp to the loom.

WEFT The material used horizontally across the warp.

SHUTTLE Weaving tool used to pass the weft through the warp.

SHED Tunnel-like opening made by lifting warp in a sequence to pass weft through. Plain weave would have every other warp raised.

BEATER Slat- or comblike tool used to move weft into place.

SELVAGES Right- and left-hand sides of weaving, parallel to warp.

BUBBLING Passing weft through warp in an arc or at a slant to prevent drawing in the selvages.

Homemade Loom

Here is an easy method to make your own inexpensive, handmade, frame loom. These are sturdy little looms that are surprisingly versatile. You can make a small loom to fit a specific purpose, such as making headbands, or a larger one for multiple purposes. Your loom needs to be at least 2" (5.1 cm) wider than the desired woven width of your project, which will make it easier to use and allow for the slight shrinkage that occurs along the selvage edges. For comfort in your lap, 18" x 24" (45.7 x 61 cm) is the maximum size you'll want to make.

SUPPLIES:

- wood, fiberboard, or hardboard of the desired size

- duct tape

- combs to span top and bottom of loom (you will need 36" [0.9 m] of combs for an 18" [45.7 cm]-wide loom)

- two 3/8" (1 cm) dowels or 1/2" (1.3 cm) flat wood trim pieces, cut to the loom width

MAKING THE LOOM

1. Cover the outer edges of the wood with duct tape.

2. Tape the bases of the combs to the wood with ½" (1.3 cm) extending past each end.

3. Tape the dowels or flat wood trim to the loom back, directly under the combs.

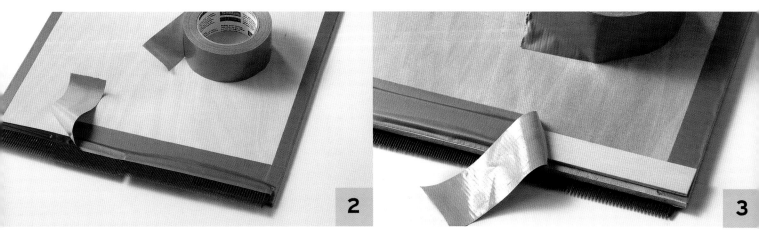

WARPING THE LOOM

1. Tie and tape the end of your warp to the loom.

2. Wind the warp up and down, wrapping it between the comb teeth. If you want lots of fringe or to continue weaving on the back of the loom, wrap the warp all the way around your loom.

3. Continue wrapping until you reach the desired width. At the end, simply tie off the end and tape it in place. Now you are ready to start weaving.

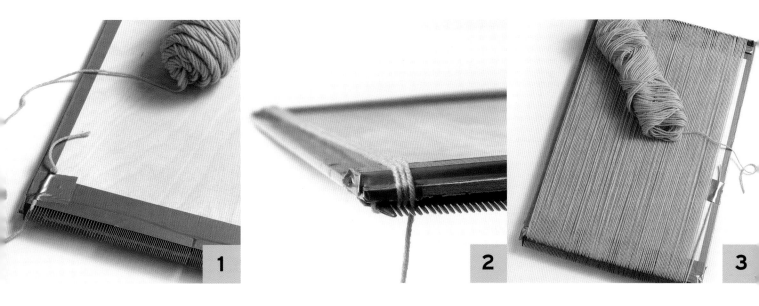

Pin Weaving

Pin weaving—where pins inserted around an outline drawing become the supports for wrapping the warp—is another way to create fabric with a specific shape. Use this method for a variety of weaving projects in all shapes and sizes, from clothing and pillows to jewelry. You can even use sewing patterns! You can create a weaving with fine details if you use a fine-gauge weaving material. When you draw your pattern, consider drawing a 1½" (3.8 cm) to 3" (7.6 cm) border at the top and bottom of your design if you want to tie off warps. You may also backstitch warp ends, which is my personal choice for the top edge since it is less bulky.

SETTING UP A PIN WEAVING

1. Tape or draw your design onto the foam core board.

2. Insert pins along the top and bottom lines of your design. Place pins close together if you want fine detail or if you will be using fine-gauge weaving material. Push pins in far enough for them to be secure but high enough to hold your warp securely while working. Tie and warp your pins.

3. Weave your design, adding in beads and stitchery details as desired. To begin and end your fibers, stitch either up or down a previously woven column next to a warp. Thread fiber tail into a needle, then insert needle tip under at least three previously woven fibers. Bring needle out to backside and trim off excess. You will work in the beginning tail after the base is woven using this same technique.

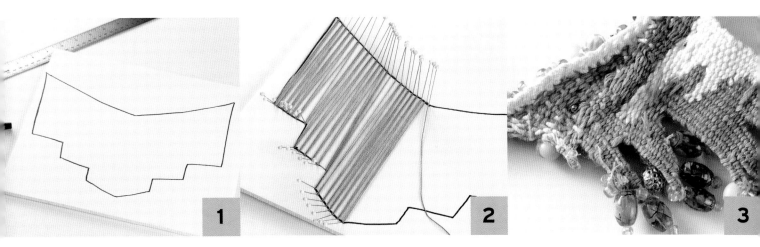

4. If you would like to add beads while weaving (which makes them appear inserted), the beads must have holes to accommodate two warp strands. To attach beads, remove a lower warp set from its pin, string on the bead, then replace warp set on pin.

5. For added stability, use liquid seam sealant on all ends and stitch around outer edges, particularly when adding the weight of beads to your weaving.

Ashford Knitters Loom

For almost seventy years Ashford Handicrafts Limited has been making the highest quality spinning wheels and looms. The New Zealand–based family business is well known for its yarns and needlework. Founder Walter Ashford responded to the need to ship spinning wheels to remote areas by designing an innovative wheel that could ship flat, assemble easily, and function perfectly for many years. Robert and Elizabeth Ashford, who now run the business, continue this spirit of innovation and quality with their latest product, The Knitters Loom.

The Knitters Loom is easy to operate. It comes with complete step-by-step instructions and photographs showing you all the details for setting it up, warping the loom, and weaving.

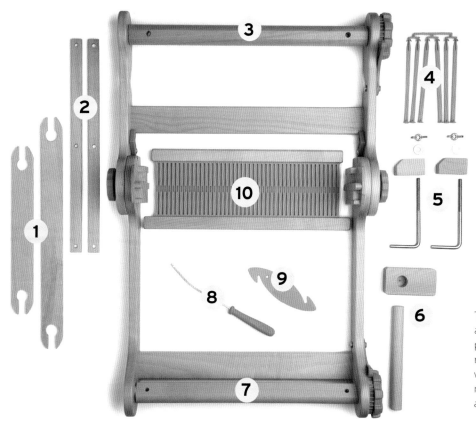

The Knitters Loom comes partly assembled and includes all of these parts: shuttles (**1**), warp sticks (**2**), back roller (**3**), warp stick ties (**4**), clamps (**5**), warping peg and peg base (**6**), front roller (**7**), heddle hook (**8**), reed hook (**9**), and reed (**10**).

The reed, which has large holes and slots to accommodate yarns, is used to create the woven fabric and to beat the rows of weaving into place. The warp threads pass through the holes and slots.

A clamp holds the loom in place as you string the warp. The warp material goes through the reed and around the warping peg, clamped to another table a set distance away. The distance is determined by how long you want your woven piece to be.

Once the loom is warped, the warp threads are wound around the back roller. Then, every other warp thread is inserted through the center hole of the reed. Once the front threads are secured to the front roller, you are ready to begin weaving.

The weft yarn is wound around the shuttle.

The reed has two positions: up and down. As the reed shifts, the warp threads separate and shift positions, creating an open space for the weft yarn.

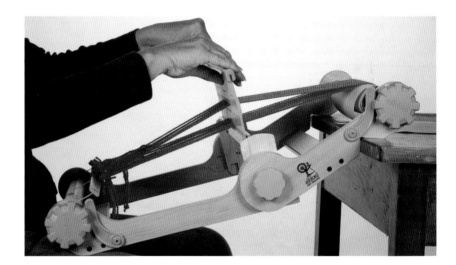

The shuttle is passed through the open space between warp yarns to create fabric.

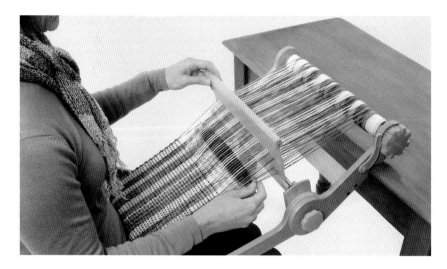

The back of the loom rests on a table while the front rests in your lap. This small loom is very versatile and can handle various weights of warp and weft materials.

It is also very portable. You can leave your project on the loom, fold it up, and take it with you.

Weavette Looms

Small handheld looms, called Weavettes, are made of varnished hardwood with stainless steel pins. They come in various sizes, including 2" (5.1 cm), 4" (10.2 cm), and 6" (15.2 cm) squares and 2" x 4" (5.1 x 10.2 cm), 2" x 6" (5.1 x 15.2 cm), and 4" x 6" (10.2 x 15.2 cm) rectangles. Two large weaving needles are included with each loom along with a detailed instruction book.

You can use Weavettes to weave small items, such as embellishments for a T-shirt, using single squares or rectangles of fabric. Or you can join two or more pieces together to create larger pieces for a wide range of projects. Using these looms is easier than it first appears—just make sure you keep the diagrams handy the first few times you use the looms and it will soon be second nature.

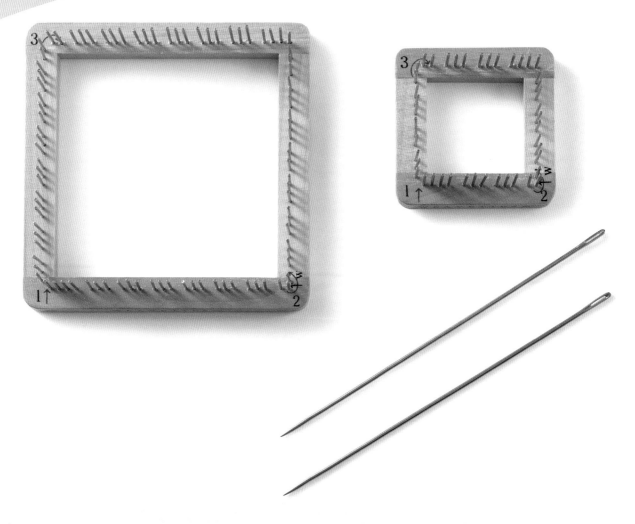

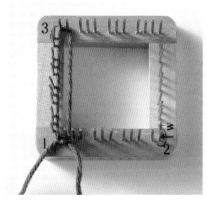

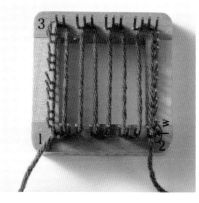

The steel pegs are arranged in sets, and the corners of the loom are numbered with arrows that keep you turning in the correct direction. To begin, tie the yarn around the first pegs on the left side.

Following the instructions and diagrams provided by the manufacturer, warp the first layer of yarn back and forth around the pegs.

Turn the loom ¼-turn clockwise and warp the second layer of yarn back and forth around the pegs.

Turn the loom back to its original position and warp the third layer.

Begin weaving, using the long needle that comes with the loom. Pass the needle alternately over and under to the opposite side.

With each pass of the needle, turn the loom a half-turn so you are always working from right to left. Continue until you reach the last row of pegs.

Tie off the thread at the corner and gently lift the fabric from the pegs.

WEAVING MATERIALS

Yarns are traditional weaving supplies and come in such a large array of colors, textures, and styles that you could weave all of your life only with yarns and never be bored! The only caveat is that, when you are first learning to weave, it is easier to keep your warp yarn taut by using a yarn with little stretch. Play around and experiment with a variety of yarns to achieve a look all your own.

Yarns and Fibers

With all the wonderful choices, it is sometimes hard to make a decision about what type of yarn to use and where. While there are no hard and fast rules, there are some things to take into consideration.

First, keep in mind that your warp will be under tension and needs to be able to withstand this tension. If you are in doubt about the strength of a yarn or fiber, take a section and pull hard on both ends. If the material easily breaks, you should choose another. Looks can be deceptive—just because a material is thick does not mean it is strong, and some very thin materials are extremely strong.

Other considerations for your choice of warp are the type of loom used, the type of weaving, and the end function of the piece. When using a commercial loom, refer to the manufacturer's instructions for advice on choosing a warp. When working on handmade looms or doing a tapestry, you will need to choose a strong warp such as cotton cable, twine, or a yarn specifically labeled for warp.

Choosing, mixing, and matching your weft materials is great fun, but keep in mind its use. For items that will be worn next to the body, consider the drape of the material and how it might feel. For home décor items, keep in mind durability as well as look and feel. If you will felt your piece, make sure to use only wool fibers. Art pieces, such as wall hangings, can incorporate just about anything.

The final consideration when choosing materials is how your warp and weft will work together. Larger, close-set warp will show more unless used with a thicker weft, while thin, wider-spaced warp is easily covered. Create a balanced weave by making warp and weft similar in size and spacing. Try twisting some warp and weft materials together to get a preview of how they might look when woven. If you are considering a large-scale project, it is always wise to weave a sample.

- Some yarns and fibers are "stickier" than others. On roller looms, try rolling warp around wax paper. On other looms, you can separate sticky fibers with smooth ones or simply work carefully.

- Try mixing different yarns and fibers together and using them as a single strand for faster weaving and (big) impact.

- Another combination to try is mixing in fabric strips, ribbon, lace, cording, twine, trims, or bead strings with yarns.

- Mix in bits and pieces from other projects. Connect by tying knots and leave the knots showing for a funky, casual look.

Try using nontraditional materials for weaving, such as string, paper, wire, hemp, fabric, plastic, and metal strips along with tubing, chain, or natural materials for a unique look. If you can get it to go through your warp, you can use it!

Estimating Materials

Estimating the amount of material needed is not an exact science because there are too many variables, such as warp and weft tension and the varying nature of every material. The exact type and shape of your loom will also affect the amount of material used. Use this only as a guide, and remember that it is always better to have a bit more material than too little—running out can be very stressful.

Each project in this book lists the type of material used and the amount in ounces and grams. The amount of material called for is what I used plus a bit extra (not much extra, but the amount I would plan on using to remake the exact same project).

Estimating Warp

To estimate warp on a commercial loom, consult your owner's manual. Please keep in mind that these, too, are only estimates. On handmade looms, multiply the number of nails or comb notches by the length of the loom. Remember to double this amount if wrapping the warp around the loom.

Basic weave
Thin material ($^1/_{16}$" [1.6 mm])—20 yd. (18.3 m)
Medium material ($^1/_8$" [3 mm])—8 yd. (7.3 m)
Thick material (¼" [6 mm])—4 yd. (3.7 m)

Soumak stitch
Thin material—32$^3/_4$ yd. (29.9 m)
Medium material—13¼ yd. (12.1 m)
Thick material—9½ yd. (8.5 m)

Rya/Ghiordes with 1" (2.5 cm) loops
Thin material—49 yd. (44.29 m)
Medium material—16 yd. (14.63 m)
Thick material—8 yd. (7.32 m)

Estimating weft based on a 4" (10.2 cm) square sample. Notice the difference depending on yarn thickness.

Tools for Applying Weft

There are a number of tools you can use to apply your weft, including yarn needles, shuttles, and butterfly wraps. Which method you will use is determined by your loom and the type of weaving.

Use a length of yarn threaded into a yarn needle for weaving in small areas or for doing more elaborate weaves. Yarn needles are also handy for working with small sheds where a shuttle will be hard to pass. Any of the projects in this book can be done with a yarn needle; some will just take much more time than they would if you used other tools.

Shuttles and bobbins are often included with purchased looms and can carry a great deal more yarn than a needle. In addition, they can make a row of weaving in a single pass, which will save you lots of time. You can also purchase additional shuttles or make your own.

To make your own shuttle, cut slits or U shapes in both ends of a thin slat of wood. Sand all edges very smooth to keep from snagging on your work.

To wind a shuttle, loop one end of the yarn around one end arm of the shuttle, then wind back and forth across the length of the shuttle. Do not wind too much yarn on the shuttle or it will be difficult to pass through the shed.

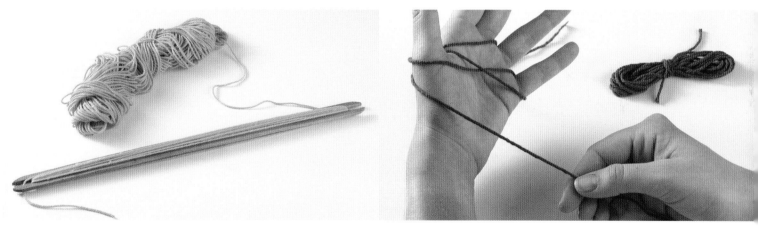

Butterfly bundles are extremely handy when working on a tapestry or rug. Using butterflies for the Rya stitch is especially useful since they easily pass around warp and over and around your dowel or stick gauge.

To make a butterfly, start by clasping the end of the yarn between two fingers. Wind the yarn around your thumb, then across the palm and around your little finger to form a figure 8. When you have wound as much yarn as you need, wrap the center with a rubber band or wrap the yarn end around the center and half hitch in place. Do not make huge butterfly bundles because they will be difficult to maneuver and can get caught in the warp.

TECHNIQUES

Warping Your Loom

If you are using a purchased loom, please follow the manufacturer's instructions. If you want some of your warp to show, then use a warp close to the same size as your weft, the horizontal fibers you will weave in. To hide your warp, use a smaller fiber, such as crochet cotton. Remember to keep the tension even.

Warp settings are referred to as ends per inch. More ends per inch are required for finer gauges of materials or finer detail in weavings. Most of the projects in this book will use eight to ten ends per inch (2.5 cm) since most use relatively bulky materials.

To warp a homemade loom follow the directions on page 11. Wind the warp up and down or all the way around your loom if you want lots of fringe or to continue weaving on the back of the loom. At the end, simply tie off and tape your end again. Now you are ready to start weaving.

Basic Weaving

Some looms and some weavers use header strips at the very beginning of their weaving. Header strips help spread the warp evenly across the loom when the warp is tied around a bar with knots. Header strips can be strips of paper, torn fabric strips, cording, or tightly woven threads. For the projects created on frame-type looms, headers are not needed; however, I recommend tamping down the first few rows as tightly as possible to stabilize the piece.

Simple Weave Patterns

There are many weaving patterns you can use on this loom, but the most common is the basic weave, or tabby, pattern—a simple over and under pattern. Make up your own variations of the basic weave by changing the number of warps you weave under and over, for example:

over 2, under 2

over 1, under 2

over 2, under 1

You will be surprised by the designs you can create with these simple patterns and combinations.

There are a number of textural and decorative stitches you can add to your weavings. Here are a few of the most common.

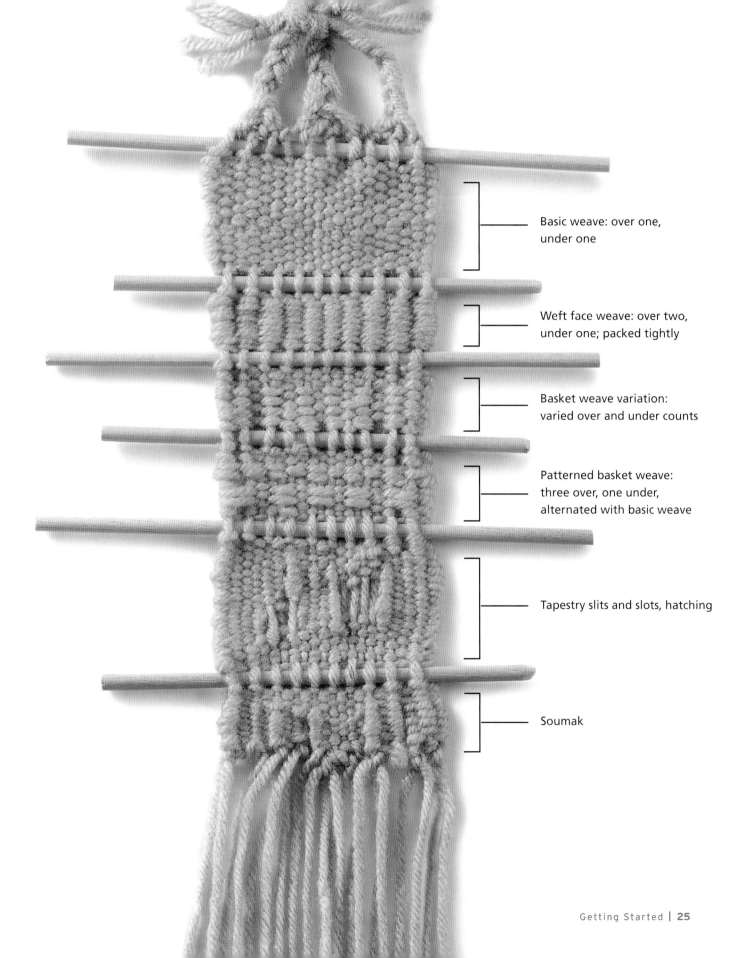

Basic weave: over one,
under one

Weft face weave: over two,
under one; packed tightly

Basket weave variation:
varied over and under counts

Patterned basket weave:
three over, one under,
alternated with basic weave

Tapestry slits and slots, hatching

Soumak

RYA OR GHIORDES KNOT

In addition to your basic weaving supplies, you will need a small dowel or slat to knot over. The size of the dowel or slat will depend on how large a loop or cut pile you desire. When designing your own weaving, you may want to try a few sizes to see which one gives the desired effect.

1. Weave several rows of basic weave before beginning this knot.

2. Bring yarn around first warp and over the dowel, then behind and over the first warp again (see top drawing at right).

3. Go over second warp, under and around the dowel. Next go under and around the third warp (see middle drawing at right).

4. When row is completed, remove dowel and pull on loops to tighten knots.

5. Weave a few rows of basic weave before adding more Rya knots. You may choose to cut the loops to make a shaggy effect (see bottom drawing at right).

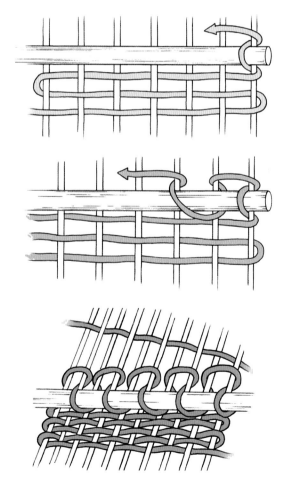

SINGLE SOUMAK

Single Soumak is a slanted, slightly raised stitch that can define areas. If you work Soumak back and forth across your weaving, the slants will run in opposite directions and create a herringbone effect. To have all slants running the same direction, work one row of basic weave in between.

1. Go over the first warp, under and around.

2. Go over the second warp.

3. Repeat.

4. To change directions, work back across row and loop around last warp. Go over next warp, under and around.

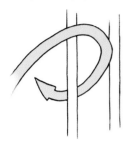
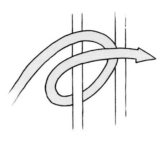
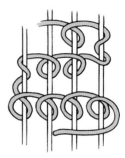

ORIENTAL SOUMAK

Another version of the Soumak is the Oriental Soumak.

1. Work as for single Soumak, except go over 4 warp, then under and around 2.

2. Repeat.

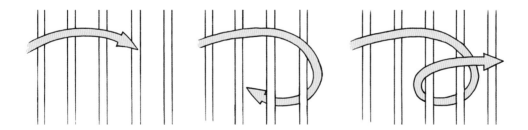

Tapestry Techniques

Weaving tapestries is an ancient art form that can be as vintage or as modern as you would like. Representational tapestries, which translate an exact image, require relatively fine fibers and a considerable amount of time. Transitional or abstract weaves are more forgiving and far easier for the novice to accomplish. Think of tapestries as painting with yarn.

There are a number of techniques you can use to translate an image to a tapestry. The most common is to draw your image onto a sheet of paper, then tape the paper to the loom under where the warp will be strung. You may also draw or paint the warp as a design guide. Using a charted grid is another common method and allows for an easy transition from other charted crafts.

The Portal Tapestry (page 96) in this book uses the Swedish method of torn paper collage, which involves gluing papers from magazines and other sources onto a paper instead of using a hand drawing. Tapestries constructed with this popular method range from transitional to abstract.

Freeform tapestries are another popular choice since they are totally reflective of the weaver. These types of tapestries are dependent on the materials used and the weave patterns or stitches. Not much preplanning is needed, but a good sense of color and style is vital. Simply begin weaving, adding in whatever material and technique you desire and letting one area flow or build upon another.

A number of techniques are used in tapestry weaving to allow color changes and decorative accents. These techniques can be added to other weavings as well, either as motifs, bands, borders, or end finishes.

SLIT

This technique produces open areas and is useful in making branches, cables, organic shapes, and elongated fringe.

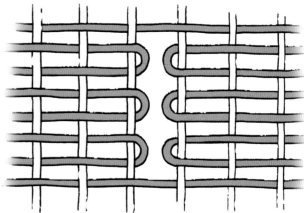

1. First, basic weave a couple of rows.

2. Weave up to the line/warp where you want the slit.

3. Weave back and forth on only these warps as many times as needed to make the size slit you desire.

4. Using a second weft, fill in the opposite side of the slit.

5. To close the slit, basic weave across the top.

INTERLOCKING

Interlocking, or dovetailing, allows different colors of weft to form a seamless finish. Done with even tension, this technique creates a slight feathered effect at the edges where the colors meet. There are three types of interlocking: vertical, diagonal, and hatching.

Vertical interlock

1. Weave the first color over to, then around a warp and back.

2. Weave the second color over and around the same warp as the first color (see top drawing at right).

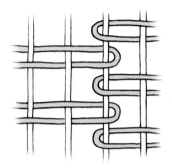

Diagonal interlock

1. Weave the first color over to, then around a warp and back.

2. Weave the second color over and around the same warp as the first and back.

3. Depending on the angle of the slant and the bulk of the yarn, you may need to repeat steps 1 and 2 to fill in the area completely (see middle drawing at right).

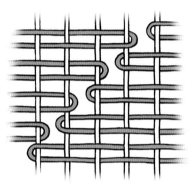

HATCHING

Hatching joins freeformed areas by interlocking the colors where they meet on a common warp (see bottom drawing at right).

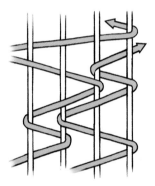

WEAVING ON A HANDMADE FLAT LOOM

To save time, you may choose to weave a wood slat through the warp following one row of your pattern. Simply turn the slat on its side to pick up all the warps in that row at one time. You may now slide the shuttle through in a single pass. You will have to go back to single picking for the next row.

1. Weave one row of your pattern, leaving a 3" (7.6 cm) yarn tail. Tamp the yarn down using your wide-toothed comb.

2. Weave the yarn tail in using the pattern for the next row.

3. Weave the next row in a slight arc and do not pull the yarn tight. Watch the sides as you tamp the yarn down again. If the yarn pulls the sides in too much, you are pulling the yarn too tight. Should this happen, make a larger arc and try holding the side the yarn is coming from between your thumb and forefinger. Tamp down as before.

SUPPLIES

- warp and weft materials
- wide-toothed comb
- shuttle or long yarn needle
- tape
- scissors
- smooth wood slat (optional)

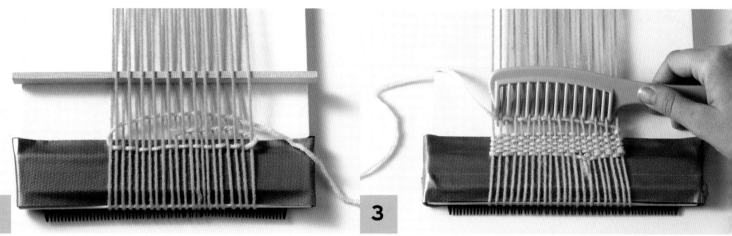

4. Continue to weave back and forth, changing patterns or yarns as you like. It is a good idea to have the weaving dense at the beginning and end of the piece to help keep the warp threads in place when you tie off.

5. To change yarns, cut the original yarn to leave a 3" (7.6 cm) tail, weave in, then add new yarn as you did to start.

6. To finish off your weaving, first weave in the last yarn tail. Place masking tape across the top and the bottom of the weaving. Now tie off each set of warp threads. Work from side to side and top to bottom to keep equal tension on the remaining warp threads. Tie two warps together in an overhand knot. You may choose to tie another row, alternating knots. (Refer to tying off and knotting section below.) Once all the warp threads are tied and removed from the loom, trim the ends as desired for fringe or weave each one into the body of the weaving.

7. Turn weaving over and trim off or weave in any yarn tails using a yarn or tapestry needle. If you are unsure about a knot or end, apply a dot of liquid seam sealant to the backside.

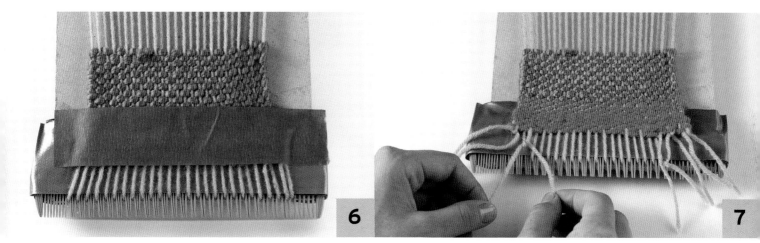

TYING OFF AND KNOTTING

Tying off your weaving securely is vital; this is what will keep your work together. How you tie off will depend on the type of material you are using and the end effect you wish to achieve. Tie smaller knots with two warps for a more refined appearance, or use square knots or more warps per knot for a chunkier, casual look.

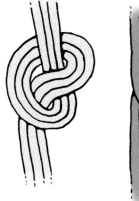
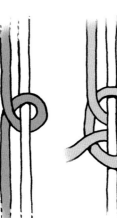
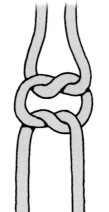

◀ Overhand knot, half hitch, double half hitch, square knot.

Finishing

Once your weaving is tied off securely, you can move on to other edge finishes. It's a good idea to know how you want to finish your weaving before you start. For example, if you decide you would like a beautiful, long beaded fringe, then you will need to allow enough warp to create the length of fringe desired. However, if you would like to finish the edges off evenly by weaving in all the ends, then you will not need as much warp (saving on material).

Part of finishing is cleaning up by taking care of any excess weft, tucking in ends, and, perhaps, clipping Rya loops. All dangling materials, aside from fringe, need to be addressed. Excess weft needs to be trimmed off or the ends woven into the body of the weaving.

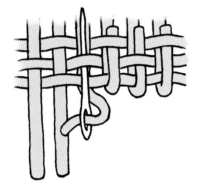

Now that your weaving is secure and tidied up it might need to be washed and/or steamed. The method used to clean your weaving depends on the materials used and, somewhat, on the end use. Wools and linens should be dipped in warm water, rinsed, and pressed while damp to shrink slightly. Synthetic fibers need only a light steaming. Tapestries, wall hangings, and rugs may need slight steaming or none at all and simply to be brushed or shaken out. Shake or brush all suede yarns and Rya areas.

Steaming will help open up the fibers and release the tension they endured during the weaving process. You will need a steam iron and press cloth. Either iron an already-dampened piece using the press cloth or set your iron on maximum steam and press with the cloth. If you are using very fluffy fibers, do not press down with the iron; hold the iron above the weaving so it just skims the surface, allowing the steam to penetrate but not flatten the fibers.

You can also express your creativity and personalize your weaving with edge finishes. The two main options are clean edge finishing by weaving in the ends (see above) and a variety of fringe techniques.

A simple, knotted fringe is perfect for many projects. Either trim warp ends off evenly or in a shape using scissors. Other ideas are to braid your fringe, macramé, add beads, wrap, or add tassels, found objects, or other items to the fringe end.

Selvage edges can be finished in a number of ways. Often you will not do any finishing along these edges. If you will be joining sections together, the edges will be finished in the joining. You might also choose to hem or crochet along the selvage.

Hemmed edges can be done on a machine (see Sewing Machines, page 35) or by hand using thread or yarn. Turn up the weaving and hem using a hemstitch.

Crocheted edges may be used on your weaving. Use a crochet hook slightly smaller than you would normally use with the weight of the material so that it can move easily through the weaving with minimal distortion. Insert your hook a few warps over from the edge to help keep your weaving in shape. Make sure to keep an even tension with your weaving by skipping over some weft rows.

CROCHET TECHNIQUES

Most people choose to hold a crochet hook as they would a pencil. The other hand will hold the work and control the yarn supply.

Slip knot

1. To begin, make a loop, insert your hook, and pull up another loop.

2. Tighten loop up next to hook.

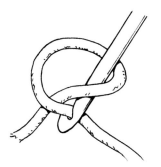

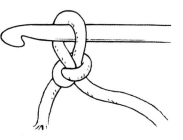

Single crochet

1. Insert hook into work, wrap yarn over the hook, then pull yarn through work only.

2. Wrap the yarn over again, then pull through both loops.

3. Wrap the yarn over the hook. Insert hook into the work.

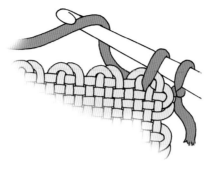

Double crochet

1. Wrap the yarn over the hook. Insert hook into the work.

2. Wrap the yarn over the hook, pull through work only, then wrap yarn again.

3. Draw yarn through the first two loops only, then wrap yarn again.

4. Draw through remaining two loops on hook.

Joining and Sewing

To join sections of weaving, decide whether you are going for a casual or refined style. If you want a casual, funky look, whipstitch the sections together with the wrong sides facing each other. This will give the seam a slightly uneven appearance. For a refined look, place right sides together, whipstitch, then turn right-side out.

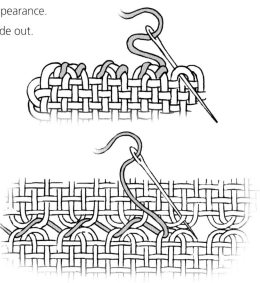

▲ Joining Weavette squares is easy too.

SEWING MACHINES

Another option for assembling your weavings is to use a sewing machine—after all, when you weave you are making fabric! Using a sewing machine gives a refined and strong seam where needed. This can be a design choice or one based on practicality. You can weave fabric and use standard sewing patterns to create whatever you like!

If you will be sewing your weaving with a machine, it is very important to consult your sewing machine manual and to make test samples. Your manual may recommend using a special needle size (I most commonly use a needle made for denim) or adjusting the tension.

Test samples help you determine the correct settings for each project and don't take very long to make. While weaving your fabric, add in an extra 10" (25.4 cm) of warp for a test sample. Place spacers between your last woven piece and the test sample to allow you to tie off easily. Weave a few inches of sample with the same materials used in your weaving. Tie off the sample with the rest of your weaving and use it to test on your machine.

Use good sewing practices such as pinning well, backstitching, and not stretching the weave as you sew. Consult a sewing book for other suggestions on sewing heavy, textured fabric or sweater knits.

EMBELLISHMENTS

On some projects you might wish to include additional embellishments, such as beading or embroidery. If you are a minimalist feel free to skip these additions, but if your philosophy is "the more, the better," then add lots more! It is totally up to you and your sensibilities.

Most of the time it is better to sew on beads with beading thread or, as in the case of the copper bracelets (page 72), wire. Keep all knots on the back of your work or hide the ends within the body of the piece. On wearable items, stitch each bead on securely and knot on the back with every other bead. On art items that will not have wear and tear, you can get by with knotting less frequently.

Standard embroidery stitches work well on weavings. Choose the size of your embroidery floss or yarn in relation to the bulk of your weaving so your stitches will show up well. Instead of knotting the end of the embroidery material, tie the ends together on the back of the weaving in a square knot. Insert the needle from back to front, make your first stitch, then insert to back and tie off.

Some handy stitches are:

Blanket stitch   Back stitch

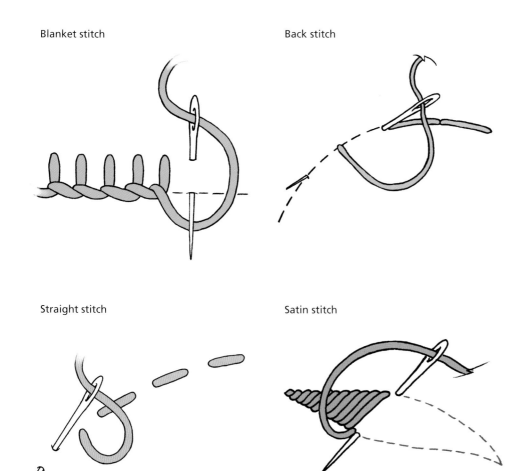

Straight stitch   Satin stitch

TIPS

- Keep your warp taut with even tension. This will make seeing where to weave easier, keep the pattern more distinct, and yield a better finished product.

- If you substitute finer-gauge weft materials, you will need more rows to cover the same distance; a larger gauge will use fewer rows.

- Make sure to tie off your weaving securely. You can use liquid seam sealant to secure slippery knots on most porous materials.

- Try various knotting patterns or adding beads to your fringe.

- Tie selvages every 3" to 5" (7.6 to 12.7 cm) to sides of frame looms to help keep them straight.

Have fun!

TROUBLESHOOTING

Warp Woes

Breaking a warp feels like a disaster, but there are a couple of things you can do to get back on track.

If you can, loosen the warp tension slightly and try to securely tie the warp back together. For extra security, dot the knot with liquid seam sealant. (This rarely works, but it's great when it does!) When you have finished weaving, weave in the knot ends.

If you are unable to tie the existing warp back together, slightly loosen the warp tension if at all possible and tie on a new section of warp, knotting securely at both ends. When you have finished weaving, weave in the knot ends.

If you have woven for a while before noticing the missing warp, you can either pull out your weaving down to the point where the warp is still attached or thread the broken warp into a needle and weave it into its rightful spot. Often, however, trying to weave a warp in is frustrating and takes more time than pulling it out and starting over from that point.

Too much tension is one of the causes of breaking a warp. To loosen tension on the Knitters Loom, just move one of the rollers. On the Weavette, you will likely need to start over from the beginning, allowing the weaving material to "lie" in between the pegs. On flat looms, you can try working with a smaller shuttle or a needle, removing the pickup stick, or pulling out the headers. If these approaches do not work, then you may need to rethink your materials or loom choice.

Too loose warp is far easier to fix than too tight warp. On the Knitters Loom, you need to just rotate one of the rollers. With the Weavette, as long as the material stays on the pegs it will probably be fine. To tighten warp on a flat loom, you can try adding some cardboard or wood slat header strips, tying off to one side, using a thicker pickup stick, or retying the warp.

Other Common Problems

Broken weft can be fixed by bringing the broken section to within 1" to 3" (2.5 to 7.6 cm) of a selvage edge. Make sure the end is snug in the weave, tamp down well, then trim off any excess. Start to weave again, securing the end of the weft.

Lumpy selvage edges are created by uneven tension, tamping, or sometimes by the material itself. Practice will help you achieve a rhythm and consistency with your weaving and cleaner selvage edges. You can hide many irregularities when you join woven pieces or sew them to other materials.

If your sides pull in, try making a bigger arc with each pass.

Loose selvage edges mean there is not enough tension. Try holding the selvage edge between your thumb and middle finger, then gently tug on the weft from the opposite side.

Treat uneven edges by crocheting along them, sewing on trims, or adding an embroidery stitch, such as a blanket stitch. You may also choose to add beading.

If, after everything is done, you are still unhappy with your piece, try one of these quick fixes: Embellish by adding found objects, beads, buttons, or even sticks and stones. Embellishments also add interest and personalize your projects, so don't be shy about using them. A well-placed button or bead can truly be the perfect solution!

I know this takes some nerve, but you can also cut apart your weaving and use it in sections to create a new project. (Remember to sew over the edges or use liquid seam sealant before cutting.) Sew blocks, strips, or a variety of shapes together to make a woven collage. Cut strips and use them to weave another piece, creating a weave on weave. You can also cut patches from less-than-perfect weavings for embellishing clothing, pillows, purses, and cases. And, finally, you can always cut down the scale of your weaving to create coasters, pockets, or small pouches and cases.

With the above skills, you can make almost anything! As your confidence grows, experiment with changing yarns or using nontraditional materials and varying your weave pattern. Let your creativity soar and make each piece a personal expression.

WEARABLES

SIMPLE SCARF

This is a great first-time project for the Knitters Loom. You will be able to whip this up in no time and get a real feel for the weaving process. The generous scarf can also be used as a stole, adding to its versatility. Crochet stitches finish the long edges. Create your own striping pattern if you wish, or use up materials left over from other projects. You will need a total of 3 oz. (85 g) of yarn for the scarf, no matter what color combinations you choose.

DIRECTIONS

1. Warp across the entire loom following the Knitters Loom warping instructions. Measure out 90" (228.6 cm) for the warping.

2. Wind the large shuttle with black yarn. Wind one side of the small shuttle with variegated yarn and the other side with lofty yarn.

3. Weave ½" (1.3 cm) black.

4. Weave 1½" (3.8 cm) variegated.

5. Weave 1½" (3.8 cm) lofty.

6. Weave 1½" (3.8 cm) variegated.

7. Weave 12" (30.5 cm) black.

8. Weave 1¾" (4.4 cm) lofty.

9. Weave 11" (27.9 cm) black.

10. Weave 1¾" (4.4 cm) lofty.

11. Weave 12" (30.5 cm) black.

12. Weave 1½" (3.8 cm) variegated.

13. Weave 1½" (3.8 cm) lofty.

14. Weave 1½" (3.8 cm) variegated.

15. Weave ½" (1.3 cm) black.

16. Tie off the warps from the loom, gathering four adjacent warps into one overhand knot tied at the base of the weaving.

17. Trim the fringed ends evenly and clip off any weft ends.

18. Double crochet along both sides of the scarf using black yarn. Crochet into every weft row.

19. Steam press the scarf if desired.

SUPPLIES

- Ashford Knitters Loom
- 2.5 oz. (71 g) black sportweight yarn
- 0.5 oz. (14 g) variegated blue/green sportweight yarn
- 0.5 oz. (14 g) lofty, nubby blue/green yarn (such as Red Heart Bright & Lofty)
- weaving tools
- size J/10 (6 mm) crochet hook

DAPPER HAT

Don't let the plaid fool you. This spiffy hat is surprisingly easy to weave because it starts as a rectangle and only needs a few hand stitches to give it a unique shape. Use the same yarn as your scarf on page 42 for a matching set. For a dash of style, make a quick and easy flower on a Weavette loom. You will need a total of 2 oz. (57 g) of yarn for the hat, no matter what color combinations you choose.

DIRECTIONS: Hat

1. Measure around head, then add 1½" (3.8 cm). This will be the length to weave (sample was woven 25" [63.5 cm]).

2. Add 30" (76.2 cm) to the measurement found in step 1. Place the warping peg at this distance.

3. Warp in the following pattern, securely tying off each warp color before changing to the next: 2 black, 6 variegated, 2 black, 11 variegated, 2 black, 11 variegated, 2 black, 6 variegated, 2 black.

4. Wind shuttles with all three yarns.

5. Weave 1" (2.5 cm) black.

6. Weave 3" (7.6 cm) lofty. If you need to adjust the height of the hat, do it here.

7. Weave 2" (5.1 cm) variegated.

8. Weave 1" (2.5 cm) black.

9. Weave 3" (7.6 cm) lofty.

10. Weave 1" (2.5 cm) black.

11. Weave 4" (10.2 cm) variegated.

12. Repeat steps 10, 9, 8, 7, 6, and 5, in that order.

13. Remove from loom, tying warps in square knots.

14. Trim the warp close and cut off any excess weft. Steam if desired.

15. Fold the hat right sides together, matching up the 12" (30.5 cm) sides. Stitch the 12" (30.5 cm) sides together using one of the yarns. You will now have a tube.

(continued)

SUPPLIES

- Ashford Knitters Loom
- 0.75 oz. (21 g) black sportweight yarn
- 1 oz. (28 g) variegated blue/green sportweight yarn
- 1 oz. (28 g) lofty, nubby blue/green yarn (such as Red Heart Bright & Lofty)
- weaving supplies
- size J/10 (6 mm) crochet hook
- yarn needle
- measuring tape
- 4" (10.2 cm) Weavette loom
- 10mm glass bead
- nine silver ball beads
- black beading thread
- beading needle

16. Fold the tube flat with the seam at one side. Stitch the top edges together.

17. Bring both upper corners to the center of the top seam and hand-tack them in place.

18. Turn the hat right-side out. Double crochet around the lower edge using black yarn.

19. Roll up bottom cuff if desired.

DIRECTIONS: Flower

1. Make 4" (10.2 cm) black Weavette square.

2. Blanket stitch around outside of square with contrasting yarn.

3. Pull one horizontal and one vertical yarn at center back of square. Pull tightly to cup and gather the flower center. Tie off pulled yarns in a knot.

4. Stitch the glass bead in the flower center, surrounded by silver beads.

5. Tack the flower to the hat.

FABRIC STRIP BELT

Use a variety of printed fabrics to create a belt for many seasons and reasons. Torn and cut strips of silk, decorator fabrics, and a mix of apparel fabrics combine to create a chameleon effect. Once you master this technique, you are on your way to all kinds of fabric strip projects. Try making rugs, cushions, placemats, runners, and purses from either new fabrics or recycled ones.

DIRECTIONS

1. Warp the loom with crochet cotton, beginning by taping down the end of the cotton in the center on one side of the loom. Wrap the cotton around the loom through the comb teeth, keeping the cotton taut and about 1/16" (1.6 mm) apart for 3" (7.6 cm). Tape down the end of the cotton even with starting point.

2. Thread a fabric strip into the yarn needle to weave. To start a fabric strip, begin in the center and weave over and under out to one edge. To secure the end, weave over and under on opposite warps below the center starting strip. Weave in a slight arc to prevent the sides from pulling in. Tamp fabric down using wide-toothed comb. Repeat over and under weaving. When 5" (12.7 cm) of fabric strip remains, weave under the last full row to the center to secure, then trim off the end.

3. Weave the entire length of the warp, mixing up fabrics and the length of the strips.

4. Cut the weaving off the loom. Cut two warps at a time even with the starting and ending points. Tie square knots with every two adjacent warps on both sides.

5. Trim any fabric strip ends.

6. Using a tapestry needle and crochet cotton, stitch a blanket-stitch around all edges to make a sturdy belt. On one end, add crochet cotton fringe to the warp ends by stitching through, knotting, and trimming all ends to 1½" (3.8 cm).

7. Slide the buckle stem through the center of the weaving 1" (2.5 cm) from the non-fringed end of belt. Fold the weaving over to enclose the buckle side, then stitch down using crochet cotton.

SUPPLIES

- ½ yd. (0.46 m) each of 5 or more fabrics, cut or torn into 1" (2.5 cm) strips
- black crochet cotton
- large, 3" (7.6 cm) belt buckle (look for these at thrift shops for a real bargain)
- lap loom (see note below)
- yarn needle
- tapestry needle
- wide-toothed comb
- scissors
- masking tape

Note: You will need a lap loom that is at least 3" (7.6 cm) wide and that is able to accommodate the desired belt length plus at least 5" (12.7 cm), or you may weave sections and join them to create the right length. Refer to Homemade Loom (page 10).

EYEGLASSES CASE

Here is a smaller version of the fabric strip technique used to create an eyeglasses case. This method makes a thick fabric that will cushion your glasses and a soft cotton lining will protect them from scratches. Decorative gold cords were woven in to give it a little sparkle; and some loopy fringe was added around the top.

DIRECTIONS

1. Weave a 3½" x 14" (8.9 x 35.6 cm) piece for the case as you did for the belt (page 48).

2. Place right sides together and use black crochet cotton to whipstitch the bottom and sides, leaving top edge open. Turn right-side out.

3. Fold the lining in half, right sides together, so you have a folded piece 4"x 7½" (10.2 x 19.1 cm). Stitch bottom and side of lining fabric together using ½" (1.3 cm) seams.

4. Insert the lining into the woven case.

5. Fold down the top edge of the lining so it is even with the top edge of the case. Slipstitch the lining in place.

6. Stitch and tie black cotton loops around the top edge by stitching into the top, looping the cotton around a finger, then making a small stitch in the same spot to lock in the loop. Repeat around the top edge to create desired fullness.

SUPPLIES

- ½ yd. (0.46 m) each of 5 or more fabrics, cut or torn into 1" (2.5 cm) strips

- 2 yd. (1.8 m) metallic cording, if desired

- black crochet cotton

- 8" x 7½" (20.3 x 19.1 cm) lining fabric, such as black cotton

- lap loom to weave 3½" x 14" (8.9 x 35.6 cm)

- yarn needle

- tapestry needle

- wide-toothed comb

- scissors

- masking tape

- sewing machine

- sewing supplies, including thread to match lining and a hand-sewing needle

SUNRISE PURSE

This quick and easy project can be made using any yarn variations or combinations you like or have on hand. The lining makes your work last longer and upgrades the project. Add a large coat button or bead to the flap, and you have a one-of-a-kind creation.

DIRECTIONS

1. Warp loom 10" (25.4 cm) using yarn A at 8 warps per 1" (2.5 cm).

2. Single basket weave (over one, under one) using yarn A for 1" (2.5 cm).

3. Switch to yarn B for 1" (2.5 cm).

4. Weave random-size stripes of yarns A, B, and C for another 14" (35.6 cm).

5. Switch to yarn B for 1" (2.5 cm).

6. Switch to yarn A for 1" (2.5 cm).

7. To weave straps, weave using all yarns for 13" (33 cm) on the 20 outside warps on both sides of the loom. Ignore the warps in center for now.

8. Remove the weaving from the loom, tying off all warps but not trimming the ends off for now. Steam finish if you would like a tighter weave.

9. For the center warps, on one end, knot and then weave in all ends. Trim off excess yarn and dot with liquid seam sealant for extra security. On the other side, knot and then braid all ends together for 3" (7.6 cm). Tie an overhand knot and pull tightly. Sew the button on top of the knot using the scrap yarn and yarn needle.

10. Line up the sides of the purse, right sides together, and slipstitch together using yarn.

11. Weave the strap warp ends in for 2" (5.1 cm). Trim off excess yarn and dot with liquid seam sealant.

12. Fold over the straps and line up the ends with the top edge of the purse. Slipstitch with yarn.

13. Sew the bottom and sides of lining fabric, right sides together, using ½" (1.3 cm) seams. Turn down ½" (1.3 cm) hem around top edge and press. If you do not have a sewing machine, use fabric glue or iron-on fusible web strips.

14. Slide lining into purse. Slipstitch lining in place along top edge using sewing thread.

SUPPLIES

- loom that will weave 9" (22.9 cm) wide by 30" (76.2 cm) long (see Tip opposite)

- 2 oz. (57 g) variegated purple, orange, red, and blue sportweight yarn (A)

- 0.5 oz. (14 g) super bulky purple yarn (B)

- 0.5 oz. (14 g) bulky, loopy variegated red, orange, yellow, and purple yarn (C)

- shuttle

- yarn needle

- large button or bead

- masking tape

- scissors

- measuring tape

- 10" x 20" (25.4 x 50.8 cm) fabric for lining, such as uses cotton print

- sewing machine

- sewing supplies including thread to match

TIP

If you would like your woven pieces to be a little larger, simply continue weaving up and over the combs and down the back. You will need to weave tightly over the combs to smooth out the weaving after it is removed from the loom. This technique is best used for small areas such as purse straps or when using variable textured yarns.

TIE-ONE-ON PURSE

Recycling has become important in our lives, and when you can recycle and make something wonderful out of it, so much the better. For this quick project, you can recycle old silk neckties into a sturdy and funky purse—no two will ever look the same. You might like to add tie tacks and clips to the purse for even more pizzazz!

DIRECTIONS

1. Prepare the ties by laundering (if desired) and removing the interfacing. To remove the interfacing, clip near the wider end to open up the center back seam, then pull out the interfacing. Smooth and flatten the ties. Choose two ties to use for your handles and set aside.

2. Warp loom with black cotton. For the Knitters Loom, set warp peg at 65" (1.7 m). Use every hole in reed, or 10 warps per 1" (2.5 cm).

3. Basic weave 8 rows using black three-ply yarn.

4. Start weaving in ties using basic weave. Place the tie in the shed, allowing the very end to extend past the sides of the warp. On the opposite side, allow the tie to make a loop before going back into the shed on the next pass. If a tie runs out mid-row, add the next tie in overlapping by ½" (1.3 cm). If the tie ends at the small end, begin the next tie at its small end (and vice versa if the tie ends at its wide end). Continue adding in ties until you have woven 30" (76.2 cm).

5. Basic weave 8 rows using black three-ply yarn.

6. Tie off from the loom using square knots with 4 adjacent warp ends.

7. Trim off excess black yarn to make even warp fringe on both ends.

8. Fold purse in half (there is no wrong side), matching up the fringed tops. Pin in place. Stitch up the sides using black yarn in a running stitch. Knot the yarn in the bottom inside corner, then work the end in between rows of tie weaving. The appearance is not important here since it will be covered later; just make sure it is sturdy.

9. Check to see if your handle ties are the same length. If they're not, trim one at the small end to match, then turn back the raw edge and glue or slipstitch in place. Place purse on a flat surface. Pin the large end of one tie to one side of the purse with the pointed end down, about 1" (2.5 cm) in from the left side. Place the narrow end of the second tie along the edge of the same side of the purse, about 1" (2.5 cm) in from the right side. Glue or slipstitch both ties in place.

10. Flip the purse over. Fold over the tie ends so they form a big loop above the top of the purse. Glue or slipstitch tie ends in place.

SUPPLIES

- Knitters Loom or homemade loom that can weave 12" x 30" (30.5 x 76.2 cm)

- heavy black cotton crochet cord or rug warp

- small amount of black three-ply yarn

- 15 to 18 silk ties

- fabric glue

- shuttle

- yarn needle

- sewing thread to match handle ties

- sewing needle and pins

- scissors

CROSSOVER CARDIGAN

Weave up this cardigan in soft cotton for warmer days and wool for those cooler days and nights. It is ideal with a camisole or T-shirt underneath or over a dress. Play with the colors, add striping, or stick to solid colors with this versatile design. Sizing is simple: for smaller sizes (8 to 10), wrap the front across, surplice style, and fasten with a belt, brooch, or sewn-on snaps. Larger sizes (12 to 14) can wear the cardigan open or pinned at the bottom of the V neckline.

DIRECTIONS

1. Set warp peg at 110" (2.8 m). Warp entire loom using white cotton.

2. Weave ½" (1.3 cm) white.

3. Weave 1¾" (4.4 cm) variegated.

4. Weave 1" (2.5 cm) blue.

5. Weave 1¾" (4.4 cm) variegated.

6. Weave 10" (25.4 cm) white.

7. Weave the next 10" (25.4 cm) white, dropping one warp on the right side on every right-to-left pass. (To drop a warp, on the left-to-right pass, stop weaving one warp before the end, then reverse direction and continue weaving as usual.) This will form the V shape at the neck of the front panel. After the weaving is 10" (25.4 cm) long, the width of your weaving should measure 5" (12.7 cm).

8. Insert 2 spacers.

9. Repeat steps 2, 3, 4, 5, and 6.

10. Repeat step 7, dropping the warp on the left side instead of the right. This forms the second front panel.

11. Insert 2 spacers.

12. Weave 19" (48.3 cm) white (one sleeve panel).

13. Remove from the loom and tie every 4 warp ends together in square knots.

14. Repeat steps 1, 2, 3, 4, and 5.

15. Weave 23" (58.4 cm) white (one back panel).

16. Insert 2 spacers.

17. Repeat steps 2, 3, 4, 5, 15, and 16 (second back panel).

(continued)

SUPPLIES

- Ashford Knitters Loom
- 1¼ lb. (567 g) four-ply white worsted weight cotton yarn
- 1 oz. (28 g) four-ply blue worsted weight cotton yarn
- 1 oz. (28 g) four-ply variegated blue/green worsted weight cotton yarn
- four 2" x 12" (5.1 x 30.5 cm) paper spacers
- steam iron
- press cloth
- sewing machine
- white sewing thread
- sewing supplies
- size C/2 (2.5 mm) crochet hook
- optional snaps for smaller sizes

18. Weave 19" (48.3 cm) white (second sleeve panel).

19. Remove from the loom and tie every 4 warp ends together in square knots.

20. Set warp peg at 82" (2 m).

21. Warp 9" (22.9 cm) of loom.

22. Weave 19" (48.3 cm) white (one sleeve inset panel).

23. Insert 2 spacers.

24. Repeat step 22 (second sleeve inset panel).

25. Remove from the loom and tie every 4 warp ends together in square knots.

26. Clip off any excess weft and remove yarn markers.

27. Steam press all pieces with a press cloth, using more steam than pressure.

28. Consult sewing machine manufacturer's instructions for advice on sewing thick materials. Make any needed adjustments for tension and needle size.

29. Pin the back panels, right sides together. Straight stitch using ³/₈" (1 cm) seam.

30. Pin the shoulder seams, right sides together, making sure the angles will form a V shape when flipped over to front. Straight stitch seams together close to the knots. Stitch again ¼" (6 mm) away from the knots. Trim off the knots, making a zigzag edge.

31. Pin one sleeve inset to each sleeve panel. Straight stitch using ³/₈" (1 cm) seam.

32. Pin one short side of sleeve unit, inset panel toward front, to cardigan with the right sides together. The sleeve seam should be 2½" (6.4 cm) in front of the shoulder seam.

33. Straight stitch seams together close to knots. Stitch again ¼" (6 mm) away from the knots. Trim off the knots, making a zigzag edge.

34. Pin the length of sleeve, under the arm, and the sides of the cardigan, right sides together, matching up the edges and border.

TIP

When weaving longer runs that will be rolled up on the front roller, tie yarn markers on the sides at even measurements before rolling them up.

35. Straight stitch using ³/₈" (1 cm) seam.

36. Trim all fringe evenly around sleeves and bottom edge. If desired, trim the fringe around the neck.

37. Single crochet both front edges. Crochet into second warp and every other weft.

38. Optional: For a surplice fit, put on the cardigan, wrapping one front panel over the other. Mark the overlap. Sew snaps to the inside of the wrap as needed.

CELL PHONE CASE

These little cases can be hooked on a belt or purse strap for easy access. Weave them using a mix of your favorite fibers. Once you get the knack, you can make versions to fit all your toting needs, such as an MP3 player case, CD holders, and knitting and cosmetics bags.

DIRECTIONS

1. Warp 4" (10.2 cm) on the loom using variegated yarn at 8 to 10 ends per 1" (2.5 cm).

2. Basket weave (one over, one under) strips of both yarns for 11" (27.9 cm).

3. Cut and knot the warp ends. Tie a second row of knots, then trim off the excess yarn.

4. Fold the weaving right sides together, with the stripes running horizontally. Use yarn needle to whipstitch sides together. Turn right side out.

5. Starting in the center of one side, single crochet around the top using variegated yarn. Crochet 2 to 3 rows depending on the size needed.

6. Chain 5" (12.7 cm). Cut yarn and knot securely.

7. Fold chain strap over the front of the case to determine where to sew on the button closure. Sew button on with yarn in desired location. Slip last chain over button to close.

VARIATION:

1. Use variegated yarn throughout.

2. Add embellished trim rows 1½" (3.8 cm) and 3" (7.6 cm) from each end.

3. Whipstitch sides together, matching up trim rows.

4. Starting 3 stitches off center at the top of one side, single crochet 2 to 3 rows.

5. Create a strap by working 5 single crochets for 5 rows. Crochet a buttonhole in the center of the strap, then finish with one final row of single crochet.

6. Fold chain strap over the front of the case to determine where to sew on the button closure. Sew button on with yarn in desired location.

SUPPLIES

- loom at least 5" wide and 12" long (12.7 x 30.5 cm)

- 0.75 oz. (21 g) of 2 or 3 different yarns, such as variegated and furry yarns

- 1" (2.5 cm) button

- yarn needle

- comb

- size J/10 (6 mm) crochet hook

- scissors

BOHEMIAN CUFFS

Wear these cuffs with any long-sleeved garment, from tees to shirts to jackets, for a fun, up-to-date take on layering. Try making cuffs from a variety of leftover yarns or adding beads or trims.

DIRECTIONS

1. Make or prepare a loom to accommodate weaving size. Refer to Looms (page 10).

2. Copy cuff pattern onto scrap paper. Tape sides together and try on to make sure the small end will fit over your hand. The small end goes inside your sleeve, with the large end folded outside, up, and over. Make any adjustments as needed, then make 2 copies of the pattern.

3. Tape the patterns to the loom with a 9" (22.9 cm) gap in between. You will be weaving both cuffs with one warping. The gap will allow you to cut the cuffs apart and still have enough yarn to knot.

4. Warp the loom with yarn A, extending the warps ½" (1.3 cm) past the long side of the pattern on both sides. Warp at 10 ends per 1" (2.5 cm).

5. Basic weave ¾" (1.9 cm) using yarn A.

6. Basic weave 1" (2.5 cm) using yarn C, then switch to a weaving pattern of 2 up, 2 down for ½" (1.3 cm).

7. Basic weave 1" (2.5 cm) using yarn B.

8. Weave a 2 up, 2 down pattern for ¾" (1.9 cm) using yarn C.

9. Weave a 2 up, 1 down pattern for ¾" (1.9 cm) using yarn B.

10. Basic weave ¼" (6 mm) using yarn C.

11. Basic weave using yarn A to complete one cuff.

12. Repeat steps 5 to 11 to create second cuff.

13. Cut cuffs off the loom, tightly knotting all yarn tails.

14. Steam finish if you would like a tighter weave.

15. On the long side, tie 2 rows of alternating square knots.

16. Dot ends with liquid seam sealant if desired. Trim any tails.

17. With the right sides together, whipstitch the sides of the cuffs together.

SUPPLIES

- loom that will weave 12" wide by 24" long (30.5 x 61 cm)
- cuff pattern (page 123)
- paper to trace pattern
- 1 oz. (28 g) sportweight variegated purple, orange, red, and blue yarn (A)
- 0.5 oz. (14 g) super-bulky orange yarn (B)
- 0.5 oz. (14 g) bulky, loopy variegated red, orange, yellow, and purple yarn (C)
- shuttle
- yarn needle
- masking tape
- scissors
- measuring tape
- liquid seam sealant, such as Fray Check

T-SHIRT EMBELLISHMENTS

Take the standard T-shirt up a few notches by adding some woven accents. Small squares woven on handheld Weavette looms can be used in various ways. Layer them, shape them into flowers, or simply leave them flat.

Flower Power Tee

DIRECTIONS

1. Stitch diagonally across the green squares, pulling in the sides to create leaves. Gather the fabric, then knot off and trim yarn.

2. Pull the center loops on the white squares to gather into a cup shape.

3. Stitch the white flower square to the green leaf square with a button in center.

4. Arrange and stitch the flower components to the shirt.

SUPPLIES

- 2" (5.1 cm) Weavette loom

- five 2" (5.1 cm) Weavette squares made from green sportweight yarn

- five 2" (5.1 cm) Weavette squares made from white sportweight yarn

- five ¼" (6 mm) yellow buttons

- sewing thread and needle

- sheet of scrap cardboard or wax paper

- fabric glue

- scissors

T-Shirt Squared Variation

Add style and pizzazz to a simple T-shirt using 2" (5.1 cm) Weavette squares. When making the Weavette squares, follow the manufacturer's instructions closely and allow the hemp to lie loosely in the loom—it will tighten up later.

DIRECTIONS

1. Place scrap cardboard or a sheet of waxed paper inside the shirt to prevent any glue seepage.

2. Place a ruler or yardstick vertically along the neck side of the shoulder seam. Use this as a guide to help you place the squares evenly down the shirt.

3. Arrange the squares on point (resembling a diamond shape) and alternating alongside the ruler or yardstick. Glue in place.

4. Allow glue to set before laundering and wearing.

VARIATION SUPPLIES

- four 2" (5.1 cm) Weavette squares made from variegated sportweight yarn

- three 2" (5.1 cm) Weavette squares made from natural hemp

- fabric glue

- ruler or yardstick

- scissors

- sheet of scrap cardboard or waxed paper

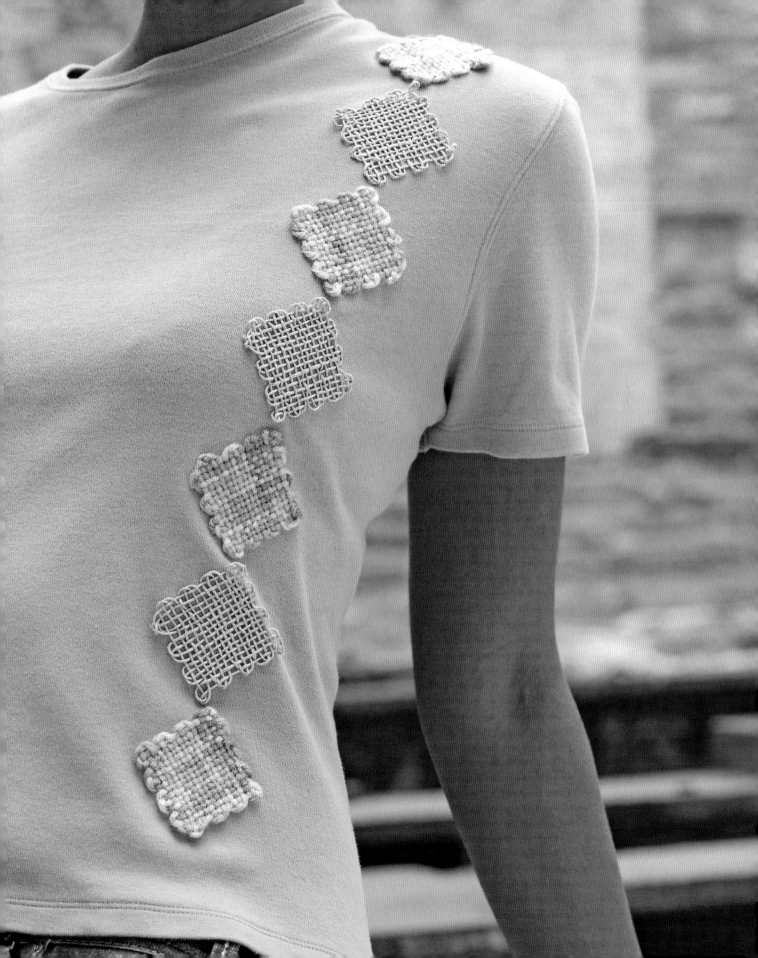

CHENILLE EAR WARMER

Weave a snuggly headband to warm your ears. Chenille yarn woven in the loopy Rya pattern (page 26) makes a wonderfully soft fabric. This circular headband is woven as a strip and joined at the back of the neck with elastic for a comfortable fit.

DIRECTIONS

1. Measure around head where headband will sit. Subtract 2" (5.1 cm) for elastic insertion.

2. Warp loom using chenille yarn. Warp at 6 ends per inch (2.5 cm) for 2½" (6.4 cm).

3. Basic weave 3" (7.6 cm) packing tightly, using chenille yarn.

4. Rya stitch one row.

5. Basic weave one row.

6. Continue alternating rows of rya and basic weave for 14" (35.6 cm).

7. Basic weave 3" (7.6 cm), packing tightly.

8. Tie off from loom. Trim off any excess weft.

9. Machine or hand stitch elastic to ends securely.

SUPPLIES

- flat loom able to weave at least 22" x 2" (55.9 x 5.1 cm)

- 2 oz. (56.7 g) chenille yarn

- ½" (1.3 cm) dowel

- 2" to 3" (5.1 to 7.6 cm) of elastic, 1¼" (3.2 cm) wide

- sewing machine or hand sewing needle with thread to match yarn

- yarn needle

- measuring tape

BEADED HEADBAND

Make this fun, quick project from textured yarn. These fashionable headbands also make great gifts or items to sell at a craft bazaar. Let your imagination run free and add all sorts of beads, buttons, charms, or combinations of yarns.

DIRECTIONS

1. Measure headband from one end to the other. Most measure 15½" (39.4 cm).

2. Warp the loom using the crochet cotton. Warp at 5 ends per 1" (2.5 cm) for 2½" (6.4 cm).

3. Basic weave 2½" (6.4 cm) using nubby yarn.

4. Weave 1½" (3.8 cm) using a 2 up, 1 down pattern.

5. Basic weave 1½" (3.8 cm).

6. Repeat steps 4 and 5 three more times.

7. Basic weave 2½" (6.4 cm).

8. Remove from loom and tie off ends.

9. Trim off excess weft. Steam press.

10. Use beading thread (doubled, if possible) to attach beads to weaving. Sew beads securely, tying knots on the back to hold.

11. Glue to headband, wrapping the ends of the weaving around the tips of the headband.

SUPPLIES

- flat loom able to weave at least 20" x 2½" (50.8 x 6.4 cm)

- 10 yd. (9.1 m) white crochet cotton

- 0.5 oz. (14 g) nubby textured yarn

- 3 flat stone beads

- beading thread and needle

- yarn needle

- purchased preformed headband

- fabric glue

- measuring tape

COPPER WIRE BRACELETS

Copper complements all skin types. Less expensive than silver, it is easy to work with and allows for different finishes from highly polished to almost black. To keep copper shiny, use wire treated to prevent tarnishing. A natural patina will develop over time on untreated copper.

Basic Copper Band

DIRECTIONS

1. Measure your wrist and subtract 1" (2.5 cm) to determine the length of the bracelet. Using this length as a guide, place 5 equally spaced nails on each narrow end of the wood base; hammer in place.

2. Warp the loom with 20 GA copper, beginning the wire around the first nail with a 1" (2.5 cm) tail extending past nail. Wrap back and forth around all nails. Wrap the end of the wire around the last nail with a wire tail extending out.

3. For both wire tails, use round-nose pliers to twist a tight loop in the wire tail. Then grasp the loop with flat-nose pliers while continuing to turn the wire in a circular path, forming the wire into a spiral that fits snugly against the nail.

4. Basic weave, beginning ½" (1.3 cm) from the nails, using 24 GA wire. Cut 12" (30.5 cm) of wire. Wrap the end tightly around one outside warp 3 or 4 times. Flatten against the warp using flat-nose pliers. Trim off the excess wire and flatten again.

5. Weave across all the warps, using the metal yarn needle to lift the warps while sliding the wire underneath. Pull the wire firmly, but not so much that you distort the warp. Use the needle to move the copper weft into place. Repeat until the weaving is ½" (1.3 cm) from the nails on the opposite end. Finish weaving and add wire as needed by wrapping wire around an outer warp, flattening, and trimming.

6. Carefully pull the bracelet off the loom. Squeeze the sides of the loop ends together slightly using flat-nose pliers.

7. Using round-nose pliers, grasp the end of the loop from the side and roll the loop toward the bracelet. Repeat on the opposite side, making sure to roll the loops to the same side of the bracelet.

8. Place the bracelet on your wrist and shape by squeezing.

SUPPLIES

- 1½" x 7" to 8" (3.8 x 17.8 to 20.3 cm) wood base for loom
- hammer
- 10 paneling nails
- 44" (1.2 m) 20 GA copper wire
- 4 yd. (3.7 m) 24 GA copper wire
- metal yarn needle
- round-nose pliers
- flat-nose pliers
- wire cutters

Beaded Flower Variation

Add a coiled wire flower and accent it with beads and a button. To create darkened copper, heat your piece briefly with a propane torch, then douse with water.

DIRECTIONS

1. Prepare loom as directed in step 1 for Basic Copper Band.

2. Warp the loom with 20 GA copper wire as directed in step 2 for Basic Copper Band, then bend wire around to start weaving without cutting the wire.

3. Basic weave loosely for the length of the bracelet.

4. Remove the bracelet from the loom.

5. Twist the wire ends together to secure. Form loops on the ends as directed in step 7 for Basic Copper Band.

6. Wind 20 GA wire around the dowel 13 times. Slide the coil off the dowel and flatten with your fingers into a flowerlike shape. Hammer the flower coil to slightly flatten it.

7. Holding the bracelet with the pliers, wave over the propane torch flame until the copper changes colors. Drop into water to cool and stop the color from changing further. Repeat with wire flower.

8. Sew the flower to the center of the bracelet using 24 GA wire. Secure the beginning of the wire by wrapping it around a woven bracelet wire on the back. Stitch over and around the flower in a few spots. Do not cut off wire.

9. Use the same wire (or, if needed, secure another wire) to sew clusters of beads to the center of the flower. String and stitch the beads as desired.

10. Stitch the button to the center of the beads. Secure the wire on the back of the bracelet.

VARIATION SUPPLIES

- 1½" x 7" to 8" (3.8 x 17.8 to 20.3 cm) wood base for loom
- 10 paneling nails
- hammer
- 20 GA wire
- 24 GA wire
- variety of green glass shard-style beads
- ⅝" (1.6 cm) copper button, shank style
- metal yarn needle
- round-nose pliers
- flat-nose pliers
- wire cutters
- ⅜" (1 cm) dowel
- propane torch

CARIBBEAN NIGHTS NECKLACE

This freeform pin-woven necklace is sure to be a show-stopper. The instructions allow you to substitute your favorite colors and beads to make your own unique creation. This is perhaps the most time-consuming project in this book, but it is well worth the time! If you want to speed things up, you can substitute a fine-gauge yarn for the floss—just remember to pack your weaving tightly to keep it stable.

DIRECTIONS

1. Copy basic necklace pattern or draw one of your own.

2. Tape or draw the design onto foam core. Place pins about every ¼" (6 mm) along the top and bottom lines and on every corner. Balance the number of pins at the top and the bottom unless you want to change the bottom edge.

3. Basic weave along the top edge using the base color. Use a fine-toothed comb or needle point to move and pack down the weaving. The weaving should be very tight and smooth.

4. Start adding in the other two colors randomly in blocks. Interlock the colors by stitching around a warp on the outer edge of the preceding color. At any point after you have completed a ¾" (1.9 cm) base, you can start to divide the weaving into branches for the fringed bottom.

5. Continue making branches and fringes until you reach the desired length. Dab liquid seam sealant on all ends and allow to dry.

6. Backstitch along the top edge using the base color. Dot the top edges and ends with liquid seam sealant and allow to dry.

7. Remove the weaving from the pins. Turn over and dot any tails with liquid seam sealant. Let dry and trim off tails.

8. Using beading thread, stitch the mixed beads along the top edge. Stitch through the weaving, add a bead, then stitch to the back. Knot frequently on the back to keep beads secure. Intersperse E beads to fill in any small spaces.

9. To stitch beads to the bottom fringe, string the beads you want to use and end with an E bead as a stopper. Insert the needle into the bead right before the E bead so that the thread wraps over the side of the E bead. Run the needle back up through all the strung beads, then stitch and knot. Repeat to decorate all fringe, dotting the ends with liquid seam sealant.

10. To determine the length of the necklace, measure around the widest part of your head and add 1" (2.5 cm). Single crochet into one end of the pin weaving, then chain until you reach the desired length. Connect the crochet chain to the opposite end.

SUPPLIES

- necklace pattern (page 118)
- 12" (30.5 cm) foam core square
- 70 to 90 pins
- 3 skeins of base color pearl cotton or embroidery floss (white in sample)
- fine-toothed comb (optional)
- 2 skeins each of 2 colors of pearl cotton or floss lime green and turquoise in sample)
- variety of beads in various sizes and shapes, including metal and E beads. You will need at least 3 packages of each glass bead style
- tapestry needle
- beading needle
- white or black beading thread
- size C/2 (2.5 mm) crochet hook
- scissors
- liquid seam sealant

KEY TO MY HEART CAMI

Make a personal statement using pin-woven patches. Pin-woven patches take little time or material to make, and they can personalize your wardrobe in a multitude of ways. This camisole has a double layer of woven hearts in two sizes with a key charm tacked into the center. Note: Sari yarn is not as easy to work with as three-ply yarn since the thickness varies and it tends to stick together.

DIRECTIONS

1. Copy heart patterns onto foam core, leaving a few inches between the hearts.

2. Starting with the large heart, push in pins every ⅛" (3 mm) all the way around the pattern outline.

3. Tie the end of the variegated yarn onto a pin in one corner of the outline. Wrap the yarn back and forth vertically across the entire heart. Tie off the end of the yarn on the pin in the corner opposite your starting pin.

4. Tie the end of the yarn through the loop formed on the pin just to left of bottom center point. Basic weave straight across to pin just right of center point. Stitch through loop on pin. Basic weave the other direction back to first pin; yarn is tied to this pin. Stitch through this loop. Continue basic weaving working back and forth across heart adding in eyelash yarn here and there by weaving it with variegated yarn. Stitch through every pin loop at least once. (If you are using very lightweight weft you may need to weave in more rows to get a solid piece. This will mean going into a pin loop more than once.)

5. You will need to work the upper lobes of the heart separately finishing one side first, cutting off yarn then tying onto other side.

6. Remove pins and then weaving. Blanket stitch around heart edges with variegated yarn working in 1" (2.5 cm) or so of yarn tails.

7. Weave and finish smaller heart in same manner using sari yarn.

8. Stitch charm to center of small heart using sewing thread or sari yarn.

9. Stack smaller heart on larger heart. Use a running stitch with sari yarn around outer edges of smaller heart to attach it to larger heart.

10. Glue or slipstitch woven patch onto shirt front.

SUPPLIES

- 8" x 11" (20.3 x 27.9 cm) foam core or very heavy cardboard

- heart patterns (page 119)

- marker

- large-headed sewing pins

- small amounts of red/orange variegated three-ply yarn, pink eyelash yarn, and sari yarn (or materials of your choice)

- small yarn needle or tapestry needle

- scissors

- brass key charm

- fabric glue or sewing thread and needle to coordinate with garment (optional)

ASHFORD SKIRT

The instructions for this stylish two-tier skirt were graciously supplied by the Ashford Knitters Loom manufacturer.

DIRECTIONS

1. With yarn A and 10-dpi reed, warp the loom to the required warp length for the finished size across the complete width of the reed (a total of 118 threads).

2. Using yarn B, weave the complete warp length.

3. Remove the finished weaving from the loom. Secure the ends with a row of zigzag stitch.

4. With yarn A and the 7.5-dpi reed, warp the loom to the required warp length for the finished size across the complete width of the reed (a total of 88 threads).

5. Using yarn B, weave the complete warp length.

6. Remove the finished weaving from the loom. Secure the ends with a row of zigzag stitch. Repeat step 4.

7. Gently hand wash both pieces with either wool wash or liquid dish-washing soap in warm water. Rinse well in warm water and either leave to dry in a rolled towel or spin out the excess water in a washing machine (spin cycle only). Smooth out the fabric and dry on a flat surface. Steam press when still slightly damp, using a damp cloth.

8. Take the 10-dpi woven piece of material and make 4 darts evenly across the full length of the top edge to fit your waist. Join the ends together with the right sides facing, sew a ½" (1.3 cm) seam, and insert the zipper using the placket method.

9. Take the 7.5-dpi woven piece and join and pin ends together with right sides facing. Sew ½" (1.3 cm) seam.

10. Make approximately 12 darts, spaced evenly around the top of the 7.5-dpi fabric piece to fit onto the 10-dpi piece.

11. Pin upper skirt over lower skirt overlapping 1½" (3.8 cm). With right sides out, sew a 1" (2.5 cm) topstitch seam to join the pieces.

12. To create the fringe, unpick the weaving up to 1 thread before the top-stitching stitch.

13. Make the lining as in step 9, without inserting the zipper.

14. Join garment and lining pieces right sides together. Sew ¼" (6 mm) seam along the top of the garment. Hand-stitch the lining to the zipper to finish. Sew the fastener at the top of the zipper for closure.

15. Turn garment right side out. Press using damp cloth. Hem lining to the desired length.

SUPPLIES

- Knitters Loom
- 2 (3, 3, 4) balls (218 yd./ 200 m; 100 g net) 100% wool yarn (yarn A) (sample uses #046 Brick Ashford Tekapo DK yarn)
- 3 (4, 4, 5) hanks (65.6 yd./ 60 m; 100 g net) rayon/ mercerized cotton (yarn B) (sample uses Yarn Traders Casablanca yarn)
- 10- and 7.5-dpi reeds
- fasteners
- sewing machine
- thread to match
- 9" (22.9 cm) closed-end zipper
- poly-cotton lining 53 (55, 57, 61)" wide (134.6, 139.7, 144.8, 154.9 cm)
- hand-sewing needle for finishing

FINISHED SIZE

36 (38, 40, 44)" (91.5, 96.6, 101.5, 111.8 cm) hip circumference. For sizes other than shown, use this formula to obtain the required warp length: Higher of waist/ hip measurement + 17" (43.2 cm) for warp ends and shrinkage = required warp length. For example, for a 36" waist/hip measurement, warp length is 36 + 17 = 53" (91.5 + 43.2 = 134.7 cm).

DÉCOR AND GIFTS

NOT-SO-70s SHAG PILLOW

This sumptuous pillow is a delight for the eyes and to the touch. Chenille, suede, and hand-dyed yarns combine with basic weave and Rya stitches to create this multi-sensory project. Rya stitches are easy but do take up time and yarn so plan on making this pillow over a couple of days. Note: Do not steam finish this project.

DIRECTIONS

1. Warp loom at 10 ends per 1" (2.5 cm) using chenille yarn. Be careful how tight you warp with this yarn, as it has a tendency to break under high stress. Warp at least 13" (33 cm) wide.

2. Basic weave using variegated suede yarn, chenille, and hand-dyed yarns in random stripes for 15" (38.1 cm). Remove from loom and tie off ends.

3. Warp loom for 2" (5.1 cm) at 8 ends per 1" (2.5 cm) using green suede yarn.

4. Basic weave 3 rows, then start Rya stitch. (See Rya or Ghiordes Knot instructions on page 26.) Alternate weaving 1 row of Rya stitches with 3 rows of basic weave for 13" (33 cm).

5. Repeat step 4 for second band.

6. Thread yarn needle with green suede yarn and sew panels together using a running stitch. Place the loopy strip so it slightly overlaps the edge of the striped panel and lies perpendicular to the stripes. Insert the needle from the back of the loopy strip up through the top of the striped panel, over ½" (1.3 cm), then back down to the back of the panel. Tie the ends together on the back. Repeat through all the layers until the entire length of the loopy strip is attached. Repeat on the opposite side with the remaining loopy strip.

7. Place the backing fabric on top of the woven piece, right side together. Pin to hold.

8. Consult the sewing machine manufacturer's guide for instructions about sewing on thick, heavy fabrics. Make any necessary adjustments. Stitch three sides together.

9. Turn right side out and fill with your choice of stuffing.

10. Slipstitch the opening closed.

SUPPLIES

- loom that will weave 12" x 15" (30.5 x 38.1 cm)

- 2 oz. (57 g) chenille yarn (sample uses olive green)

- 2 oz. (57 g) suede yarn (sample uses olive green)

- 0.5 oz. (14 g) variegated suede yarn (sample uses burgundy/blue/green)

- 0.25 oz. (7 g) hand-dyed variegated yarn of varying thickness

- 15" x 18" (38.1 x 45.7 cm) backing fabric (sample uses green moleskin)

- fiberfill or quilt batting for pillow stuffing

- shuttle

- yarn needle

- masking tape

- scissors

- measuring tape

- sewing supplies including sewing machine, pins, needles, and sewing thread to match backing

COZY UP

You'll say "no, thanks" to cardboard sleeves when you have your own chic hand protector. This cup cozy fits cups up to 11" (27.9 cm) circumference, but can be easily adapted to fit coffee mugs and commuter mugs. If you need a larger circumference, weave it separately using 3" (7.6 cm)-wide warp x desired size plus 20" (50.8 cm).

DIRECTIONS

1. Set warp peg at 65" (165.1 cm) to create teapot cozy and one cup cozy. Add 10" (25.4 cm) for each additional cup cozy.

2. Warp across loom using yarn A.

3. Weave 1" (2.5 cm) using yarn A.

4. Weave 1" (2.5 cm) using both yarns B and C in each pass.

5. Weave ½" (1.3 cm) using yarn A.

6. Weave ¾" (1.9 cm) using yarns B and C.

7. Weave 20" (50.8 cm) using yarn A.

8. Repeat steps 6, 5, 4, and 3, in that order.

9. Insert cardboard spacers. This will allow you to easily tie off both the teapot cozy and the cup cozy.

10. Weave ½" (1.3 cm) yarn C.

11. Weave 1" (2.5 cm) yarn A.

12. Weave ½" (1.3 cm) yarn C.

13. Remove both pieces from the loom, tying every 4 warp ends into a square knot.

14. Trim the fringe evenly and cut off excess weft.

15. Set your iron to steam wool. Place the press cloth over both weavings. Steam press lightly to tighten up the weave.

16. Fold the tea cozy in half along its length, matching up the border on both sides. Stitch sides together. Turn right side out.

17. Measure 2" (5.1 cm) down and 6" (15.2 cm) in from one side. Thread the yarn needle with 2 strands of yarn C. Stitch over 2, under 3 all the way around to create a drawstring. If a few warp before you reach the starting point again, stop and bring the needle out to the front. Pull the drawstring to gather up the top of the cozy; tie in a bow.

18. Stitch the button to one short end of the cup cozy. Slide the cozy around the cup, opening up the weave for the button to pass through.

TEAPOT COZY SUPPLIES

- Ashford Knitters Loom
- 3.5 oz. (99 g) yarn A (Lion Wool and Fun Fur is used here)
- 0.75 oz. (21 g) variegated yarn (yarn B)
- 0.5 oz. (14 g) eyelash yarn (yarn C)
- weaving tools
- yarn needle
- iron
- press cloth
- sewing supplies
- size C/2 (2.5 mm) crochet hook
- optional snaps for smaller sizes

CUP COZY SUPPLIES

- 0.5 oz. (14 g) yarn A
- 3 yd. (27.4 m) each of other yarns
- ⁵⁄₈" (1.6 cm) button
- two 1½" x 12" (3.8 x 30.5 cm) light cardboard strips (for spacers)

AUTUMN SUNSET TABLE RUNNER

This project mixes wool with acrylic yarn—not always the best idea! When mixing these two types of yarn, you must be careful when steam finishing and accept that there will be some unevenness between the two types of yarn due to the wool shrinkage. In this case, I really liked the effect. If you would rather have completely even surfaces, substitute wool for the nubby yarn. Adjust the length of the table runner by clipping the fringe short or by keeping it long. For this sample, I tied an alternating square knot pattern in the fringe for a netting effect.

DIRECTIONS

1. Set warp peg at 90" (2.3 m). Warp entire loom using variegated four-ply wool.

2. Basic weave 2" (5.1 cm) using solid wool.

3. Weave one row of single Soumak using solid wool.

4. Basic weave ½" (1.3 cm) using nubby yarn.

5. Basic weave 1" (2.5 cm) using solid wool.

6. Basic weave 2" (5.1 cm) using nubby yarn.

7. Basic weave 1" (2.5 cm) using solid wool.

8. Basic weave ½" (1.3 cm) using nubby yarn.

9. Weave one row of single Soumak using solid wool.

10. Basic weave 1" (2.5 cm) using solid wool.

11. Basic weave 3" (7.6 cm) using variegated wool.

12. Basic weave 10" (25.4 cm) using solid wool.

13. Basic weave 6" (15.2 cm) using variegated wool.

14. Basic weave 10" (25.4 cm) using solid wool.

15. Basic weave 3" (7.6 cm) using variegated wool.

16. Basic weave 1" (2.5 cm) using solid wool.

17. Weave one row of single Soumak using solid wool.

18. Basic weave ½" (1.3 cm) using nubby yarn.

(continued)

SUPPLIES

- Ashford Knitters Loom

- 4 oz. (113 g) solid color four-ply wool yarn (sample uses Rose Lion Wool)

- 5 oz. (142 g) variegated four-ply wool yarn (Autumn Sunset Lion Wool Prints is used here)

- 2 oz. (57 g) nubby, variegated yarn (Lion Homespun Corinthian is used here)

- yarn needle

- scissors

- iron with press cloth

19. Basic weave 1" (2.5 cm) using solid wool.

20. Basic weave 2" (5.1 cm) using nubby yarn.

21. Basic weave 1" (2.5 cm) using solid wool.

22. Basic weave ½" (1.3 cm) using nubby yarn.

23. Weave one row of single Soumak using solid wool.

24. Basic weave 2" (5.1 cm) using solid wool.

25. Remove weaving from loom and tie off ends using an overhand knot on every 2 adjacent warp.

26. Trim off excess weft and weave in ends.

27. Dip weaving into warm water mixed with a small dab of liquid soap. Agitate gently and rinse well. Squeeze out the excess water, but do not wring. Let weaving partially dry on a flat surface. Iron using a press cloth. Allow to dry completely.

28. Tie alternating square knots on the fringe ends. To do this, tie overhand knots close to the weaving using 4 adjacent strands (two of the overhand knots you first made to secure the weaving after removing it from the loom). Tie the first row of square knots using 8 strands from 2 adjacent overhand knots. Four strands will be in the center with 2 strands on each side for knotting. Place the square knot 1" (2.5 cm) below the overhand knots. Tie a second row of square knots 1" (2.5 cm) below the first row using 4 strands from 2 adjacent knots from the first row.

29. Trim fringe evenly.

RUSTIC TABLE RUNNER

With a little imagination, some very unusual materials can be used in your weaving projects. For this rustic table runner, sisal twine alternates with cotton yarn to create both the warp and the weft. Common wooden rulers and thin reeds make interesting weft insertions. This conversation piece can also be used as a wall hanging. If you hang it vertically, you may want to fringe only one end.

DIRECTIONS

1. Set warp peg at 88" (223.5 cm).

2. Warp 4 sisal, 5 yarn, 2 sisal, 7 yarn, 8 sisal, 7 yarn, 2 sisal, 5 yarn, and 4 sisal.

NOTE: For this project, do not use the loom reed except to hold the warp. Sisal will fray and snag on the reed; however, using the loom rollers will keep the work manageable. You may use a pickup stick to insert the weft in one direction.

3. Basic weave is used throughout. Weave 1½" (3.8 cm) yarn.

4. Weave a reed. Insert the reed as if it were a yarn pass.

5. Weave ½" (1.3 cm) yarn.

6. Weave 2" (5.1 cm) sisal.

7. Weave a ruler.

8. Weave 2" (5.1 cm) yarn.

9. Weave a reed.

10. Weave 2" (5.1 cm) yarn.

11. Weave 2" (5.1 cm) sisal.

12. Weave a ruler.

13. Weave 2" (5.1 cm) yarn.

14. Weave a reed.

15. Repeat steps 12, 13, 14, 15, and 16 three more times.

16. Weave 1½" (3.8 cm) yarn.

17. Remove from loom and tie off ends using overhand knots with every 4 adjacent warps.

18. String 1 bead on every 4 warps. Slide every other bead (high beads) up next to the weaving, then tie an overhand knot directly underneath it to hold it in place. Allow the alternate beads to rest just below the high beads. Tie an overhand knot under them to secure them.

19. Due to the loose weave, the reeds and rulers tend to slip. On the back of the runner, dot the reeds and rulers with fabric glue to secure.

SUPPLIES

- Ashford Knitters Loom

- ball of sisal twine

- 1.5 oz. (43 g) nubby cotton yarn

- six 14" (35.6 cm) reeds

- five 1" x 12" (2.5 x 30.5 cm) thin wood rulers or slats

- forty-two 20mm natural wood barrel beads

- fabric glue (optional)

ABSTRACT TAPESTRY

Turn photos, graphics, or even fine art prints into personalized weavings using tapestry techniques. With extremely fine-gauge weaving materials, warping at a high number of ends per inch (centimeter), and some patience, you can get a realistic copy. But with a little imagination, you can also do an interpretation like this abstract tapestry. Draw with a marker around the major design elements, then copy just those outlined elements onto another sheet of paper. Color your sections with crayons, pencils, or markers. Use this cartoon to guide your weaving adding texture for more pizzazz. Make your own or use my pattern.

DIRECTIONS

1. Tape the pattern to the loom, making sure the outlines are clear. (You may choose to outline each section with colored markers so they are easier to see.)

2. Warp across loom at 10 ends per 1" (2.5 cm). If using a small hand-made loom, warp around the loom so you will have more fringe at the end.

3. Weave in all sections, following the directions for tapestry techniques on page 27. This is also a good place to try various weave patterns.

4. Remove weaving from loom and tie off ends with overhand or square knots.

5. Tie washers randomly to bottom fringe.

6. Screw nuts onto the ends of the rod. Tie the top of the hanging to the metal rod using double half hitches.

7. Gather up a few yarn leftovers, push through the weaving, then tie in a knot on the back.

VARIATION IDEAS:

- Work this same pattern in a monochromatic color scheme.

- Work the pattern using any other color scheme. Choose one from a favorite fabric or a favorite room of your house, or use any three adjacent colors on the color wheel.

- Turn the pattern on end.

- Add beads, found objects, or buttons.

SUPPLIES

- pattern (page 120)

- loom able to weave 8" x 10" (20.3 x 25.4 cm)

- ribbon-type yarn for warp (sample uses dark blue)

- less than 1 oz. (28 g) each of the following yarns:

  dark blue textured
  red/orange mixed texture
  purple/blue mixed texture
  blue tones mixed texture
  white three-ply
  green three-ply
  yellow three-ply
  turquoise three-ply
  red, orange, and yellow variegated

- yarn needle

- comb

- pencil

- 9" (22.9 cm) long 1/8" (3 mm) threaded metal rod with 2 nuts to match

- variety of metal washers from 1/4" (6 mm) to 1/2" (1.3 cm)

PORTAL TAPESTRY

For this project, you may choose to follow the pattern, or try the Swedish method of torn paper collage. For the torn paper collage method, you will need to gather a variety of papers, a glue stick, and a copy of the pattern. Tear the paper into sections and glue onto the pattern. The torn paper collage method allows you to try out color combinations in advance and get a pretty good idea of what the finished piece will look like.

DIRECTIONS

1. Enlarge the pattern to desired size or make a torn paper collage as a guide. Tape to the loom under the warping area. It is very helpful to make a second copy of the pattern to refer to as you weave.

2. Warp the loom at 12 ends per 1" (2.5 cm) using cotton warp.

3. Insert the cardboard strip as a header.

4. Basic weave 6 rows using warp thread.

5. Weave 3 up, 1 down for 6 rows using brown three-ply yarn.

6. Refer to the pattern and to the Tapestry Techniques section (page 28) to weave in the remaining sections using a variety of yarns and stitches. For a more durable piece that can be laundered, hatch or interlock sections together.

7. Weave 3 up, 1 down for 6 rows using brown three-ply yarn.

8. Basic weave 6 rows using warp thread.

9. Remove from loom and tie off the ends using an overhand knot on every 4 warp.

10. Add foliage to the tree shape using the dark sage and variegated green yarns. Stitch from the top down, over a warp, then bring back to the top and knot. Trim ends. Repeat until foliage reaches desired fullness.

11. Weave in ends and trim off excess weft.

12. Lightly steam tapestry.

13. To attach to a jacket, pin in place, then slipstitch around the edges, allowing the bottom fringe to hang free.

SUPPLIES

- pattern (page 121)

- loom able to weave 11" x 22" (27.9 x 55.8 cm)

- ecru rug warp or heavy crochet cotton

- less than 1 oz. (28 g) each of the following yarns (or any colors you wish), all acrylic or acrylic blends:

  brown three-ply
  brown variegated nubby
  green three-ply
  green variegated three-ply
  light sage green three-ply
  dark sage green three-ply
  gray/blue three-ply
  blue textured
  light gray three-ply
  dark gray three-ply
  beige/white variegated suede
  beige/ white variegated nubby

- 1½" x 12" (3.8 x 30.5 cm) strip of cardboard

- yarn needle

- comb

- pickup stick (optional)

WOVEN MATS FOR PHOTOS OR ART

Add the texture of woven material behind your favorite photograph, bead, button, or memorabilia for an extra spark. These are quick, easy, and can jazz up everything from albums to wall art.

You Rule! Photo Mat

DIRECTIONS

1. Use the saw to cut the measuring stick into two 4" (10.2 cm) sections, two 2½" (6.4 cm) sections, and one 5" (12.7 cm) section with a hole on one end. If your measuring stick is not ¾" (1.9 cm) wide, you will need to adjust the 2½" (6.4 cm) pieces to fit.

2. Glue the two 4" (10.2 cm) sections and the two 2½" (6.4 cm) sections of the measuring stick around the sides of the black hemp mat using the multi-surface adhesive. Allow the glue to set.

3. Glue the 5" (12.7 cm) measuring stick section across the center back of the mat, extending past the top, with the hole on top. The hole will allow you to easily hang this piece.

4. Glue the photo in place on the front of the mat.

Tribal Intrigue Photo Mat Variation

DIRECTIONS

1. Glue the wrong side of the fabric to the frame backing. Spread the glue evenly and smooth the fabric to avoid wrinkles. Allow the glue to dry. Trim off any excess fabric around the backing edges with scissors.

2. Stitch the bead to the center diagonal of the woven square using yarn or, if the bead hole is small, beading thread.

3. Glue the beaded square to the fabric-covered backing on the diagonal.

YOU RULE! SUPPLIES

- small saw or heavy-duty utility knife

- 18" (45.7 cm) vintage or new wood measuring stick (sample is $^3/_4$" [1.9 cm] wide)

- 4" (10.2 cm) black hemp Weavette square

- multi-surface adhesive (such as Gem-Tac)

- photo to fit mat

TRIBAL INTRIGUE VARIATION SUPPLIES

- 4¾" x 6¼" (12.1 x 15.8 cm) black frame with 3" x 4½" (7.6 x 11.5 cm) opening

- 4" x 5" (10.2 x 12.7 cm) print fabric

- fabric glue

- scissors

- 1" (2.5 cm) bone bead

- needle that will fit through bead

- 2" (5.1 cm) turquoise yarn Weavette square

MOD TEDDY

This teddy is quite extraordinary with his soft suede yarn body, flamboyant bow tie, and anime-inspired silhouette. He can be made without contrasting tummy and muzzle for an entirely different character. You will need to weave fairly tightly to give strength to the fabric, so remember to use a pickup stick to save some time.

DIRECTIONS

1. Enlarge the pattern 200% and tape it to the loom base. It is helpful to work with 2 copies so you can place the pattern on top of the weaving now and then to check accuracy

2. Warp the loom at 10 ends per 1" (2.5 cm) using brown sportweight yarn.

3. Basic weave as directed in the diagram, using suede yarn up to the belly.

4. Weave belly area in a 3 up, 1 down pattern using nubby yarn.

5. Continue basic weave with suede yarn, interlocking (page 29) where intersecting with the belly area. Weave up to muzzle area.

6. Weave muzzle in a 3 up, 1 down pattern using nubby yarn.

7. Continue basic weave with suede yarn, interlocking where intersecting with the muzzle area.

8. Optional: Dot short warp areas with liquid seam sealant; allow to dry.

9. Backstitch around the warp between the head and the arms where the warp ends are short.

10. Tie every 4 warps off from the loom using square knots.

11. Weave the back of the teddy in the same manner, deleting the belly and muzzle area. Place the completed front on the weaving now and then to check accuracy.

(continued)

SUPPLIES

- teddy pattern (page 122)

- flat loom able to weave at least 14" x 20" (35.6 x 50.8 cm)

- shuttle or yarn needle

- comb

- 2 oz. (57 g) four-ply brown sportweight yarn

- 2 oz. (57 g) variegated beige/brown suede yarn

- 0.5 oz. (14 g) nubby beige yarn for belly and muzzle

- 2 yd. (1.8 m) four-ply black yarn for eyes and nose

- 10 yd. (9.1 m) red four-ply yarn

- pickup stick (optional)

- liquid seam sealant, such as Fray Check (optional)

- 5 handfuls of fiberfill

- size H/8 (5 mm) crochet hook

12. Use black yarn to satin stitch the eyes. Straight stitch from the top edge of the muzzle center down 1" (2.5 cm). Insert the needle from front to back, then back up to the top of the muzzle and over ¼" (6 mm). Insert the needle through to the front, crossing over the first muzzle line and over ¼" (6 mm) to complete the nose.

TIPS

- It is better to weave a bit past the pattern outlines rather than be short of fabric later. If you "over weave," it is easy to tuck any excess fabric into the seam.

- On warp with short ends that are hard to tie, you can dot them with liquid seam sealant close to the weaving. Let it dry, then backstitch around each warp before cutting.

13. Place the front over the back, wrong sides together. Blanket stitch around all edges using brown sportweight yarn, tucking in warp knots as you go. Leave opening along one side.

14. Stuff teddy with fiberfill. Finish the stitching at the opening.

15. Crochet the bow tie using red yarn: Chain 6. Double crochet rows until the strip is 18" (45.7 cm) long. Tie the strip around teddy's neck in a knot.

ASCENSION SCULPTURE SHADE

Artistic weaving as a sculptural form, where the loom becomes part of the finished piece, has existed for eons in the form of baskets. You can make loom bases from all kinds of existing forms, such as the inexpensive floral easel used in this project. Once you start looking around for forms to weave on it is hard to stop! I used double-sided paper for this sample, but you can use any sturdy paper such as watercolor, wallpaper, or even fabric mounted onto paper. If you don't have your own strips of photo negatives, you can buy them online and at garage sales, or you can use vellum or stencil plastic.

DIRECTIONS

1. Stand easel upright. Measure 22" (55.9 cm) on each leg and mark. Use a hacksaw to trim each leg. File off any rough edges.

2. Follow the manufacturer's instructions to spray paint the easel black. Allow the paint to dry.

3. Work the wire directly off the spool. Start stringing up one triangle side by winding the end of the wire around the top of the wire form. Twist the wire around itself, then wind around the form a few more times (see illustration opposite). Wind the wire from top to bottom of the triangle side, wrapping twice around the form on each end.

4. Wrap so there are 24 wires on each side. Wrap the end of the wire around the top several times to secure. (Do not worry about how the top looks; it will be covered later.)

5. Use the paper trimmer or the straightedge, knife, and mat to cut several ¾" (1.9 cm) strips from 2 of the papers.

6. Weave the first 10" (25.4 cm) in a basic weave (see instructions below) over and under single wires. Combine 2 wires for each weave after that since the wires are very close together. Basic weave 2 sides in the following pattern:
   - paper strip, bamboo skewer to outside of frame. Repeat 5 times.
   - negative strip, bamboo skewer to outside, paper. Repeat 2 times.
   - bamboo skewer, paper.

7. On third side, weave in the same pattern except place every other skewer to the outside of the frame.

8. Use scissors to trim the paper ends on a diagonal and the skewers just past the sides of the frame.

9. Trace the cap pattern onto the third paper and cut it out. Fold the cap and glue along the seam. Place on top of the frame.

10. Set up the low-voltage light fixture, if using, to illuminate the artwork.

SUPPLIES

- 24" (61 cm) wire floral easel (sold with floral supplies)
- measuring tape
- hacksaw
- metal file
- black spray paint
- 30 yd. (27.4 m) 24 GA silver wire
- paper trimmer or straight-edge with craft knife and cutting mat
- three pieces 12" x 12" (30.5 x 30.5 cm) double-sided paper in coordinating prints (such as scrapbook paper)
- 9 negative film strips
- 33 bamboo skewers
- scissors
- snips or pruning shears to trim bamboo
- cap pattern (page 124)
- paper glue
- 15-watt free-standing light fixture (optional)

AMULET BAGS

From start to finish, an amulet bag takes less than an hour to make—a little more if you make your own beaded fringe instead of using the premade by-the-yard variety. If you want, you can use fabric glue instead of needle and thread to hold the sides and attach the beaded trim.

Each amulet bag uses only one kind of yarn. The color changes in the blue, cranberry, purple, and teal bag are created by the variations in the yarn. There are many other ways to vary the colors within an amulet bag: Yarn is wound around the loom in three directions before being threaded into a needle for the fourth side, woven over and under to hold the layers together. This means you can use up to four different colors or textures in a single rectangle, producing horizontal or vertical stripes as well as a host of other patterns.

DIRECTIONS

1. Weave rectangle using yarn of choice. Remove from loom.

2. Fold rectangle up 1½" to 2" (3.8 to 1 cm) to form a pocket (this measurement determines the length of the front flap) and sew at the sides. Fold down the flap.

3. Sew or glue beaded trim to flap and/or bottom of bag. Sew or glue accent bead to flap.

4. Tie together three 1¼" yd. (1.14 m) pieces of yarn with overhand knots at approximately 3" (7.6 cm) intervals. Sew or glue to sides of amulet bag.

Note: Adjust the length of the hanging cord as desired, but make sure it is long enough to go over the person's head if the amulet bag will be worn as a necklace.

SUPPLIES

For both bags:

- Weavettes loom, 2" x 6" (5.1 x 15.2 cm)

- purchased beaded trim, accent bead, or other embellishments

- needle and sewing thread (or fabric glue)

Green bag:

- green worsted weight yarn for woven rectangle and 1 strand of the hanging cord (sample uses Moda Dea Eclipse, Art. R154 Color 2567, Nile Green)

- green 90% acrylic yarn with beads and silver thread for 2 strands of the hanging cord (sample uses Moda Dea Beadnik, Art. R149 Color 2917, Groove Green)

Blue bag:

- variegated yarn for woven rectangle and all 3 strands of the hanging cord (sample uses Moda Dea Sassy Stripes, Art. R105 Color 6250, Crayon)

WEAVING IN THE MARGINS

Albums, altered books, journals, and art pieces made from hardbound book covers can be as diverse as their creators. Make them simple and elegant, reflect the title, or go all-out funky; it's up to you. Find sturdy, hardbound books with interesting covers at thrift stores and use up leftover bits of yarns, lace, and fibers to make these inexpensive, creative projects. There a few ways to make these covers, depending on the end purpose:

Method 1

Use chalk to draw lines for the tacks (refer to the samples for two different layouts). Nail in the tacks, allowing the tack ends to penetrate the book.

Method 2

For an art piece to place on an easel or hang on a wall, use a utility knife to cut the cover off the book. Use chalk to draw lines for the tacks (refer to the samples for two different layouts). Cut wood slats the width of the tack lines to keep the tack ends from coming through. Nail in the tacks through the covers and into the slats.

Method 3

Follow method 1, then use wire cutters to cut off the tack ends. Glue cardstock to the inside cover.

Window Weaving

DIRECTIONS

1. Hammer in 9 tacks at the top and the bottom of the book cover. Hammer in 5 tacks at the top and the bottom of the center area (around the title or picture).

2. Tie on and warp using crochet cotton.

3. Basic weave rows of all yarns, fibers, and lace, allowing the ends to extend out both sides. Tie the ends together close to the weaving and let the ends drape down in random lengths. Repeat until you reach the bottom row of center tacks.

4. Weave up the sides of the center using variegated yarn.

5. Weave the top and the bottom in a variety of yarns and fibers.

SUPPLIES

- hardbound book cover with central title or picture, prepared using desired method

- hammer

- 28 carpet tacks

- tan crochet cotton for warp

- small amounts of a variety of white- and beige-toned yarns and fibers, including white chenille, variegated suede, and white eyelash

- 2 to 3 yd. (1.8 to 2.7 m) of 1/2" (1.3 cm)-wide white lace

- yarn needle

- scissors

Full Cover Weaving Variation

This is a freeform weaving; the overall effect is of trees in the foreground.

DIRECTIONS

1. Hammer 16 tacks at the top and the bottom of the cover.

2. Tie and warp using black crochet cotton.

3. Basic weave using black sportweight yarn to create a hill shape 1" (2.5 cm) tall on the right side and up to 3" (7.6 cm) tall on the left (you will skip over warps as you work up to the 3" [7.6 cm] side).

4. Create tree trunks using black crochet cotton on a set of 4 warps on each side. Make branches of random thickness and lengths as you work up the sides. Weave between 6 and 8 rows of trunk between branches. Use your needle to arrange the branches, but keep in mind that tying on foliage will secure them later. Make both trees in this manner, varying their size and shape from each other.

5. Tie variegated yarns onto the trunks and branches. Stitch into the trunk, tie the ends together, then trim closely. On the branches, tie around the warps to secure and align branches as you add foliage.

6. Glue trim, if using, to the bottom edge of the weaving. Bring the ends around to the back and glue in place.

VARIATION SUPPLIES

- hardbound book cover with central title or picture, prepared using desired method as directed on page 108

- 32 carpet tacks

- black crochet cotton for warp

- small amount black sportweight yarn

- yarn needle

- small amounts of 2 variegated yarns in fall foliage colors

- scissors

- hammer

- metal embellished trim 2" (5.1 cm) wider than cover (optional)

- fabric glue (optional)

ARROYO BRANCH HANGING

This monochromatic freeform piece has a strong rustic feel. Make the loom for your hanging from branches, wire, and screws (you can also lash the corners together). Relating the woven leather in the belts to the weaving gives the piece continuity.

DIRECTIONS

1. Stack the top and bottom branches over the side branches at the corners to form a frame. Drill through the top branch and partway into the bottom one. Screw in the wood screw. Repeat in all corners.

2. Cut about 2 yd. (1.8 m) of wire (more for large branches). Securely wrap the wire around the branch intersection in one corner, wrapping in both diagonal directions.

3. Warp the branches using the jute twine. Tie the end of the jute to one upper branch corner with a half hitch, then a square knot. Wrap 3 times around the opposite branch, then bring the jute back up to the first branch. Wrap 3 times, then down to the opposite branch. Repeat at least 32 times across branches.

4. Determine where you will place the belts, then start weaving them in using basic weave. You may choose to wrap the ends of the belts around the side branches or trim them off 1" (2.5 cm) past the body of the weaving. Trim the belts using heavy duty scissors or leather shears. Apply a line of fabric glue to the back of all the trimmed belts to keep them from unraveling (unless you like that look). If you want to wrap the belts around the side branches, trim the belts long enough to wrap around branch plus 3" (7.6 cm). Use fabric glue on the back to secure belt ends. Use clothespins to clamp belts until fabric glue sets.

5. Stabilize the weaving by basic weaving jute for a few rows. Pack down tightly with your comb. You may choose to use a shuttle for the first part of the weaving and then switch over to butterfly wraps (page 23) as the working area gets smaller and the warp gets tighter.

6. Continue weaving with jute and yarn, using tapestry techniques (page 28) to make freeform shapes with slits. Comb organic shapes, exposing the warp here and there. Comb down the weaving securely around all shapes.

7. Weave in more belt sections as desired.

8. Weave the top portion of the hanging using jute and yarn. On the next-to-last row, do a single Soumak stitch. Weave the final row and tuck in the ends.

9. Turn the weaving over and tie off and trim long weft.

10. Wrap and tie additional jute around the upper corners, if desired.

SUPPLIES

- 4 branches approximately 27" (68.6 cm) long
- 4 wood screws 1/4" (6 mm) shorter than branches when stacked
- measuring tape
- drill with drill bit matching wood screws
- screwdriver
- 10 yd. (9.1 m) black/gray 18 GA utility wire (sold in hardware stores)
- wire cutters
- needle-nose pliers
- 400 yd. (365.6 m) spool of three-ply jute twine
- scissors
- 4 or 5 woven natural leather belts
- craft scissors or leather shears for cutting belts
- fabric glue
- clothespins
- comb
- 1 oz. (28 g) ivory/beige textured yarn
- shuttle

WHIRLPOOL

Weave a spiraling circle of fibers into a whirlpool of Caribbean waters. The dynamic shape and graphic contrasts of this art piece add to its energy. This sample was woven on a 23" (58.4 cm) bicycle rim, but you can use large metal rings or wood hoops instead. Often you can find inexpensive rims at thrift stores, garage sales, or junk dealers. After removing the spokes, rims make great frame looms.

Weaving on a bicycle rim does present some challenges. When you warp across the diameter, the warps lie on top of each other in the center and are wide apart near the edges. A center medallion, found object, or grouping of fibers can cover the center. On the edges you can stitch a laced design, use bulky groups of fibers, finish the design before the warp spreads too far, or use any combination of these techniques. As you work from the inside out you will need to secure your yarn tails by sliding them under previous rows to clean finish the weaving (page 32).

DIRECTIONS

1. Disassemble the rim to remove the spokes and the hub (most can be disassembled using wrenches). Clean well and sand or file any rough edges.

2. Tie the warp securely to rim through one spoke hole using a double half-hitch followed by a square knot.

3. Run the warp across the rim to the opposite side and in through the spoke hole to the outer rim. Bring the warp over to the adjacent spoke hole, then in and across to the opposite side. Repeat for all spoke holes, filling the rim with warp running across the inside of the rim. Tie off securely.

(continued)

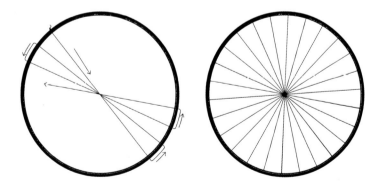

SUPPLIES

- 23" (58.4 cm) bicycle rim

- black three-ply cable cotton

- black duct tape (or any color to coordinate with rim color)

- 2 oz. (57 g) nubby blue/green yarn

- 2 oz. (57 g) variegated blue, silver, and white ribbon fiber

- 2 oz. (57 g) lime green bulky yarn

- 1 oz. (28 g) turquoise three-ply yarn

- $1\frac{1}{2}$ oz. (43 g) black three-ply yarn

- $1\frac{1}{2}$ oz. (43 g) variegated blue/green three-ply yarn

- yarn needle

- scissors

4. Tear strips of duct tape just slightly narrower than the rim width. Press the strips down inside the outer rim cavity, covering the warp as they move from spoke hole to spoke hole.

5. Start weaving in the center, going over and under multiple warps. Use a combination of fibers and yarns with Rya stitching worked over a pencil. Work the center 2½" (6.4 cm) in this manner.

6. Weave sections of warp using single yarns and fibers in basic weave. Create slits at random (see Tapestry Techniques, page 28).

7. Continue weaving, hatching in at times and creating more slits and mixing fibers together. Once you are about 4" (10.2 cm) out from the center, start adding in multiple strands of yarns and fibers in each woven section. Secure yarns and fibers by stitching up through previously woven columns (see Finishing, page 32).

8. When weaving the last few rounds near the edges, stitch a single Soumak stitch.

9. Add laced edging by securing the black yarn to the woven base. Stitch a half hitch around the base of the warp next to the weaving, then stitch another half hitch on the adjacent warp next to the rim. Repeat around the entire weaving/rim.

10. Soumak stitch around the weaving using a bundle of 8 yarns and fibers, going over and around the Soumak stitch next to the weaving.

11. Secure the black yarn to the warp next to the rim. Wind the yarn over the rim, under and around the upper black Soumak stitch, then back up to the rim. Bring the yarn over and around the rim, going in between next to the adjacent warp. Repeat all around, then tie off securely.

Caribbean Nights Necklace

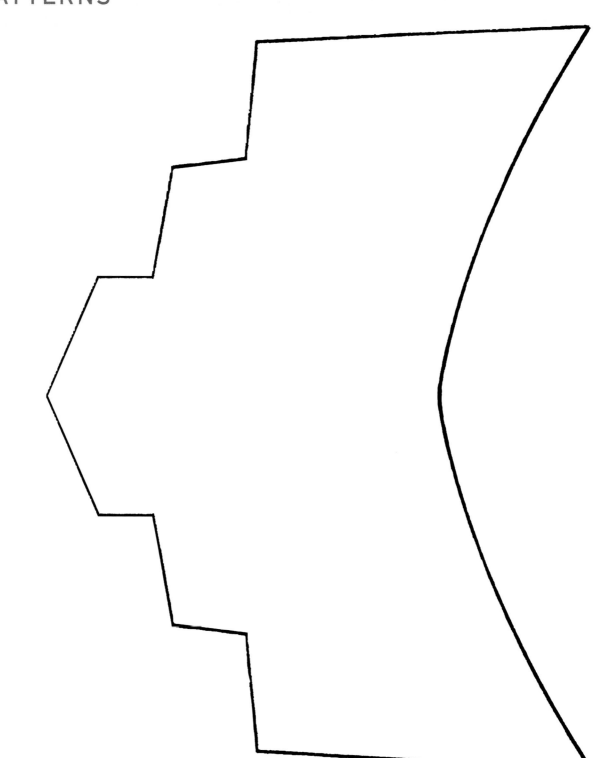

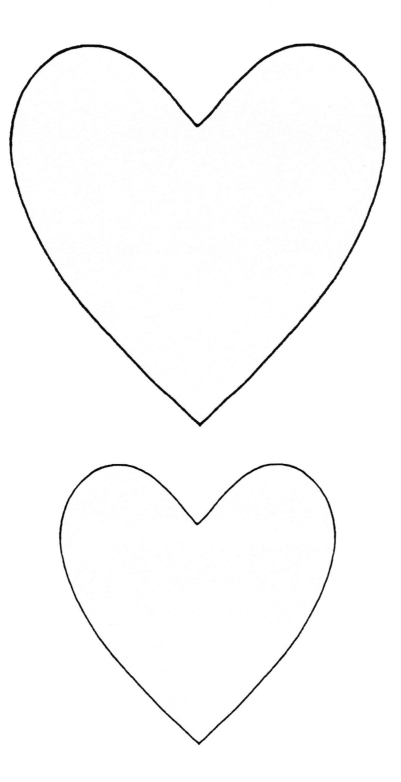

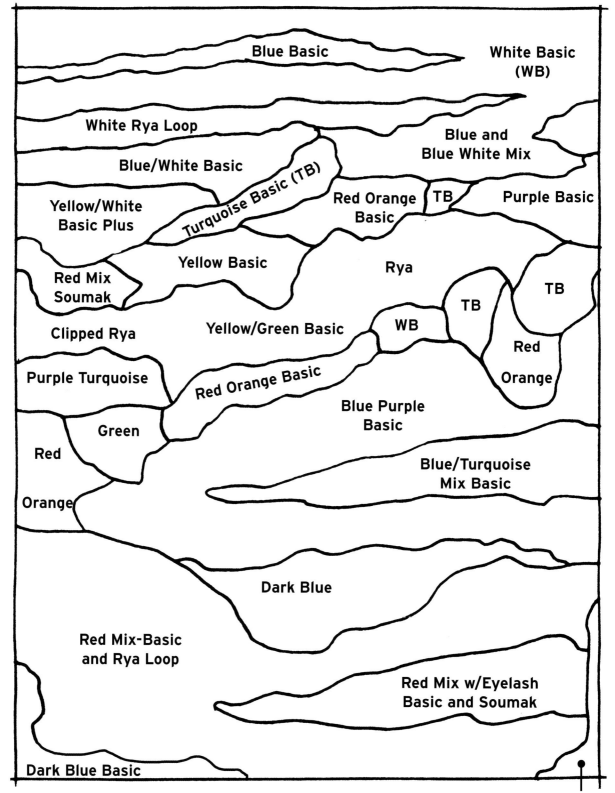

Abstract Tapestry - Enlarge 130%

Blue Basic

White Basic
(WB)

White Rya Loop

Blue and
Blue White Mix

Blue/White Basic

Turquoise Basic (TB)

Red Orange
Basic

TB

Purple Basic

Yellow/White
Basic Plus

Yellow Basic

Rya

TB

Red Mix
Soumak

TB

Red
Orange

Clipped Rya

Yellow/Green Basic

WB

Purple Turquoise

Red Orange Basic

Blue Purple
Basic

Green

Red

Blue/Turquoise
Mix Basic

Orange

Dark Blue

Red Mix-Basic
and Rya Loop

Red Mix w/Eyelash
Basic and Soumak

Dark Blue Basic

Dark Blue Basic

Mod Teddy - Enlarge 200%

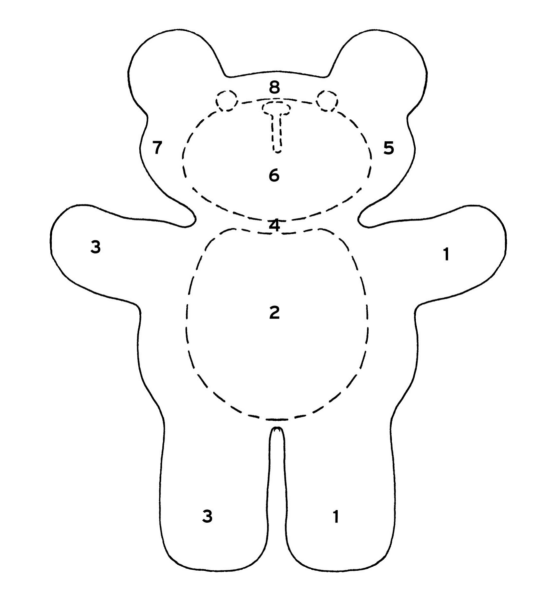

Bohemian Cuffs

Ascension Sculpture Shade

Score & Fold   Cut

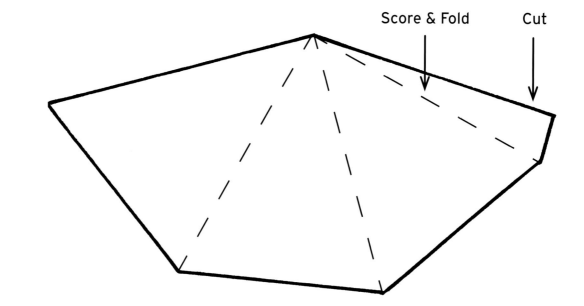

RESOURCES AND SUPPLIERS

ASHFORD LOOMS

New Zealand
Ashford Handicrafts Limited
PO Box 474, Ashburton
Phone: +64.3.308.9087
Fax: +64.3.308.8664
Email: sales@ashford.co.nz
www.ashford.co.nz

Australia
Ashford Australia Pty Limited
Travellers Rest, The Four Mile
583 Snowy Mountains Highway
Cooma, NSW 2630
Phone: +61.2.6452.4422
Toll-Free: +1.800.026.397
Fax: +61.2.6452.4523
Email: ashfordaustralia@bigpond.com
www.ashfordaustralia.com

Austria
Wiener Webwaren
A-1210 Wien, Kainachgasse 19/3/5
Vienna
Phone: +43.1.292.7108
Email: info@wienerwebwaren.at
www.wienerwebwaren.at

Canada
Harmonique Spinning Wheels & Looms
P.O. Box 50038
15-1594 Fairfield Road
Victoria, B.C.
V8S 5L8
Phone: +1.250.294.4411
Toll Free: +1.877.294.4411
Fax: +1.250.294.8411
Email: info@harmonique.ca
www.harmonique.ca

Chile
Sociedad Commercial Wisniak
Santiago
Phone: +56.2.556.9221
Fax: +56.2.551.6519
Email: losalata@interaccess.cl
www.costuritas.cl

Czech Republic
DALIN Praha s.r.o.
Rezlerova 281
10900 Praha 10
Phone: +420.274.860.304
Fax: +420.274.860.304
Email: linhartova@dalin-praha.cz
www.dalin-praha.cz

Denmark
Skytten
4871 Horbelev
Phone: +45.5444.5020
Fax: +45.5444.5022
Email: mail@skytten-danmark.dk
www.skytten-danmark.dk

Spindelvaeven
Brændeskovvej 15
5800 Nyborg
Phone: +45.6611.1499
Email: vibe@spindelvaeven.dk
www.spindelvaeven.dk

France
Ets Marie Saint Germain
9, rue du Capitaine Flayelle BP69
88203 Remiremont
Phone: +33.03.29.23.00.48
Fax: +33.03.29.23.20.70
Email: contact@artifilum.com
www.artifilum.com

Germany
Monika Traub
Schorndorfer Str. 18
73650 Winterbach
Phone: +49.71.81.70.91.0
Fax: +49 71.81.70.91.11
Email: moni@traub-wolle.de
www.traub-wolle.de

Holland
The Spinners
Den Haag
Phone: +31.7.0397.3643
Email: info@despinners.nl
www.despinners.nl

Japan
Ananda Co., Ltd.
1221 Nagasakashimojyo
Nagasaka-cyo, Hokuto-shi
Yamanashi 408-0025
Phone: +81.0551.32.4215
Fax: +81.0551.32.4830
Email: wool@ananda.jp
www.ananda.jp

Craft Hitsujiza
Fukuoka-shi
Phone: +81.92.8511.358
Fax: +81.92.8511.358

Mariya Handicrafts Limited
Sapporo
Phone: +81.11.221.3307
Fax: +81.11.232.0393
Email: koichi-m@ra2.so-net.ne.jp

Ocean Trading Co., Ltd
Kyoto
Phone: +81.75.314.8720
Fax: +81.75.313.6150
Email: green@oceantrading.co.jp
www.oceantrading.co.jp/spinning

Sanyo Trading Company Limited
Ibaraki
Phone: +81.297.78.1000
Fax: +81.297.78.5850
Email: adx01490@ams.odn.ne.jp

Malaysia
Multifilla (M) Sdn BHD
No 1, Jalan 2/2,
Taman Industri Selesa Jaya,
Balakong, 43300 Selangor Darul Ehsan
Phone: +603.8961.3686
Fax: +603.8961.3637
Email: mfilla@tm.net.my
www.multifilla.com

Norway
Spinninger
Billingstad
Phone: +47.66.84.60.22
Fax: +47.66.84.60.22

Korea
LDH Hand Weaving Loom
Fine Corp., Ltd
Seoul
Phone: +82.02.2266.0207
Fax: +82.02.2272.1378
Email: finecenter@finecenter.com
www.finecenter.com

South Africa
Campbell Crafts & Marketing
Cape Town
Phone: +27.21.686.6668
Fax: +27.21.448.8506
Email: campbellcrafts@netactive.co.za

Sweden
Gudruns Ullbod
Enkoping
Phone: +46.171.399.95
Fax: +46.171.399.96
Email: ullbod@gudrunsullbod.com

Switzerland
Spycher-Handwerk
Huttwil
Phone: +41.629.62.1152
Fax: +41.629.62.1160
Email: info@spycher-handwerk.ch
www.spycher-handwerk.ch

Taiwan
Founder Tek Int'l Co Ltd
Taipei
Phone: +886.2.2.781.1699
Fax: +886.2.2.751.2521
Email: foundtwn@ms12.hinet.net
www.foundertek.com.tw

United Kingdom
Haldanes Craft and Tools Ltd
2/3 Bellman Way
Donibristle Industrial Park
Dalgety Bay
Fife
KY11 9JW
Phone: +44.1383.821406
Fax: +44.1383.825331
Email: haldanesltd@aol.com
www.haldanes.co.uk

United States
Foxglove Fiberarts Supply
8040 NE Day Road W, Suite 4F
Bainbridge Island, WA 99110
Phone: +1.206.780.2747
Fax: +1.206.780.2848
email: sales@foxglovefiber.com
www.foxglovefiber.com

WEAVETTE HANDHELD LOOMS

United States
Buxton Brooke Looms
1382 West Main Street
Williamstown, MA 01267-2625
Phone: +1.800.358.2782
www.weavettes.com
Use the website to find a retailer near you.

ABOUT THE AUTHOR

Barbara Matthiessen's design work covers a wide range of styles and mediums. She particularly likes to mix things up by combining traditional materials in innovative ways or by using nontraditional materials with standard techniques. It's all about experimenting and enjoying the experience.

Barbara has a specialized degree from an interior design school and worked for a design firm before entering the industry as a full-time freelance designer. She has written three books and forty-three booklets, has contributed to twenty-two multi-artist books, and has done countless designs for magazines. While continuing to design for publication, she works for manufacturers as well, developing kits, project sheets, and sales models. She also teaches varied technique classes at art retreats around the country.

Barbara lives in the Pacific Northwest with her husband, Larry. They enjoy their grandchildren and trailer camping whenever they get a chance.

INDEX